THE MARSHALL CAVENDISH
★ ★ ★ ILLUSTRATED ★ ★ ★
ENCYCLOPEDIA OF
WORLD WAR II

VOLUME 13

THE MARSHALL CAVENDISH ☆ ☆ ☆ ILLUSTRATED ☆ ☆ ☆ ENCYCLOPEDIA OF

WORLD WAR II

Based on the original text by
Lieutenant Colonel Eddy Bauer

CONSULTANT EDITOR

Brigadier General James L. Collins, Jr., U.S.A.

CHIEF OF MILITARY HISTORY,
DEPARTMENT OF THE ARMY

MARSHALL CAVENDISH CORPORATION/NEW YORK

CONTENTS

Editorial Director: Brian Innes
Editor-in-chief: Brigadier Peter Young, D.S.O., M.C., M.A.
Managing Director: Richard Humble
Editor: Christopher Chant
Art Editor: Jim Bridge

LIBERATION

CHAPTER 120
The tension grows

△ The British advance–past the grave of a German soldier.

The unsavoury gossip about Bradley was nothing to the criticisms made of Montgomery regarding the mediocre victories which the British 2nd Army could claim at that time. It had in fact to attack three times, and it was not until July 9, 1944 that it was able to announce the capture of Caen, its D-Day objective.

Of course, Montgomery could hardly reveal to the journalists whom he gathered round him for periodical press conferences that he had no intention of opening up the route to Paris. Still less could he tell them that his plan aimed first and foremost at forcing Rommel to concentrate his Panzers against the British 2nd Army, and wearing them down on this front by a series of purely local actions. Having said this, however, it may be said that in this battle of equipment, Montgomery the master-tactician did not sufficiently bear in mind the

enormous technical superiority that German armour enjoyed over the British and American tanks. If we look again at accounts of the furious battles fought out in the Caen sector in June and July, 1944, all we seem to read about is Sherman tanks burning like torches, Cromwell tanks riddled like sieves, and Churchill tanks, whose armour was considered sufficiently thick, never surviving a direct hit. Here, for example, is part of Major-General Roberts's description of Operation "Goodwood" on July 19 and 20.

"But 3 R.T.R. were through. They had started with 52 tanks, been given 11 replacements, making 63 tanks in all. With Bras now in their hands, they had nine tanks left. Major Close's A Squadron had lost 17 tanks in two days, seven being completely destroyed, the others recoverable; all Troop officers had been killed or wounded, and only one troop Sergeant was

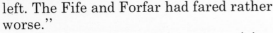

△ *British Shermans in open country. By maintaining the strongest possible pressure on the Caen front, Montgomery planned to pull the bulk of the German armour away from the American sector of the front.*

left. The Fife and Forfar had fared rather worse."

In the circumstances it is not surprising that the famous units that had formed part of the 8th Army in North Africa (the 50th and 51st Infantry Divisions, and the 7th Armoured Division) did not have the success expected of them in this new theatre of operations. Writing of these veterans of Bir Hakeim, Tobruk, and El Alamein, Belfield and Essame remind us of the old saying current in the British Army—"An old soldier is a cautious soldier, that is why he is an old soldier." Quite probably. But perhaps the hiding the Desert Rats received at Villers-Bocage on July 12, when they first came into contact with the 2nd Panzer Division, was such as to make even the most reckless prudent.

As for the 12 British divisions which came under fire for the very first time in Normandy, however realistic their training may have been, however keen they may have been to fight, the real thing was very different, and the conditions they were called upon to face in real combat sometimes took away some of their aggressiveness.

It is also possible to criticise the British High Command for the tendency in its instructions to try to foresee everything, even the unforeseeable. Having seen orders issued by the main American commanders, we know that they subscribed to the same theory as the Germans, that the order should contain all that the lesser commander needs to know to carry out his task but nothing more; whereas British orders tended to go into further detail, limiting the initiative of the tactical commanders, because of theoretical situations that did not always arise. For in war, it is said, it is the unexpected that happens.

In this list of Montgomery's resources, an honourable mention must be made of the artillery, for which Rommel's grenadiers had a special dislike, for it fired quickly and accurately. In particular, the 25-pounder "gun-howitzer" fired so rapidly that the Germans thought it must have been fitted with a system of automatic loading. And this fact goes a long way to explain the form which the fighting took in the Caen sector, for if the British tanks

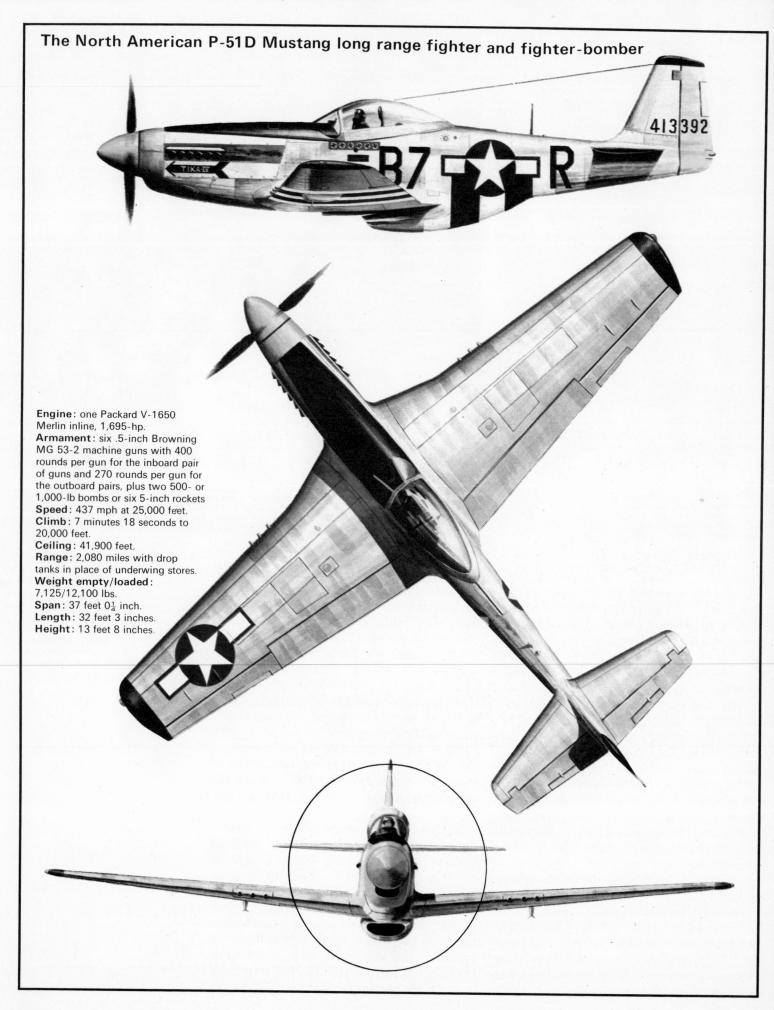

The North American P-51D Mustang long range fighter and fighter-bomber

Engine: one Packard V-1650 Merlin inline, 1,695-hp.
Armament: six .5-inch Browning MG 53-2 machine guns with 400 rounds per gun for the inboard pair of guns and 270 rounds per gun for the outboard pairs, plus two 500- or 1,000-lb bombs or six 5-inch rockets
Speed: 437 mph at 25,000 feet.
Climb: 7 minutes 18 seconds to 20,000 feet.
Ceiling: 41,900 feet.
Range: 2,080 miles with drop tanks in place of underwing stores.
Weight empty/loaded: 7,125/12,100 lbs.
Span: 37 feet $0\frac{1}{4}$ inch.
Length: 32 feet 3 inches.
Height: 13 feet 8 inches.

◁ *A British patrol pushes into the ruins of Caen.*
▽ *The Cassino of France. What was left of Caen.*

failed in all their attempts at break-through whenever they came up against the German Panthers, Tigers, and the 8.8-cm anti-tank guns of *Panzergruppe* "West", the German counter-attacks collapsed under the murderous fire of the British artillery concentrations whenever they went beyond purely local engagements. All the more so since at that distance from the coast the big guns of the Royal Navy were able to take a hand. So it was that on June 16 in the region of Thury-Harcourt, about 20 miles from Riva-Bella, a 16-inch shell from the *Rodney* or the *Nelson* killed Lieutenant-General Witt, commanding the 12th S.S. Panzer Division "*Hitlerjugend*".

The failure of British XXX Armoured Corps and the 7th Armoured Division to turn the front of *Panzergruppe* "West" at Villers-Bocage seems to have caused Montgomery to shift the centre of gravity of his attack to the countryside around Caen, where his armour would find a more suitable terrain.

Operation "Epsom", begun on June 25, brought into action VIII Corps, just landed in Normandy and commanded by Sir Richard O'Connor, released from captivity by the signing of the Italian armistice. Covered on his right by XXX Corps' 49th Division, O'Connor was to cross the Caen–Bayeux road to the west of the Carpiquet aerodrome, push on past the Fossé de l' Odon, then switching the direction of his attack from south to south-west, he would finally reach Bretteville-sur-Laize, ten miles south of Caen, near the Caen–Falaise road. This would give the British 2nd Army not only the capital of Normandy, but also the Carpiquet air base, upon which Air-Marshals Coningham and Leigh-Mallory had long been casting envious eyes.

VIII Corps had 60,000 men, 600 tanks, and 700 guns. The 15th and 43rd Divisions, each reinforced by a brigade of Churchill tanks, provided O'Connor with his shock troops, whilst the 11th Armoured Division would then exploit the situation. For all three divisions it was their first taste of combat.

Whilst the left wing of XXX Corps attacked the Panzer-*"Lehr"* Division, VIII Corps' attack brought it into contact with the 12th S.S. Panzer Division *"Hitlerjugend"*, commanded, since the death of General Witt, by General Kurt Meyer, a leader of extreme resolution, of rapid and correct decisions, whom his men had nicknamed "Panzer-Meyer". By nightfall, at the price of fierce combat and despite incessant counter-attacks, the British infantry was able to bed down near the Caen–Villers-Bocage road, three miles from their starting point. On June 27, the 15th Division managed to capture a sound bridge over the Odon, and the 11th Armoured Division advanced and began the switching movement mentioned earlier: the first objective was Hill 112, the summit of the ridge which separates the Odon and Orne Valleys.

German counter-attack fails

The VIII Corps, however, was now behind schedule, and some very troublesome bottlenecks were building up at its rear. These difficulties enabled Sepp Dietrich, commanding I S.S. Panzer Corps, to avoid the worst by bringing in General Paul Hausser's II S.S. Panzer Corps, which had just come back from the Galician front. He even tried to take the 11th Armoured Division in a pincer movement between the 9th S.S. Panzer Division *"Hohenstaufen"* and the 10th S.S. Panzer Division *"Frundsberg"* and only failed because O'Connor evacuated his troops from a salient that had become too exposed.

On the other hand the *Panzergruppe*

"West" failed in its efforts to turn this defensive success into a general offensive, for II S.S. Panzer Corps was literally pinned down by artillery fire and tactical air bombardment whenever it made the slightest move. In this connection General Harzer, Chief Operations Staff Officer of the 9th S.S. *Panzergrenadier* Division said later: "Now, if the Luftwaffe had been able to deal with the Allied navies and also stop the accurate bombing of certain targets, I think that the British-Canadian landings would once again have 'fallen in the ditch', as they say. As it was, our counter-offensive broke down under air attack and artillery fire, particularly the heavy guns of the battleships. They were devastating. When one of these shells dropped near a Panther, the 56-ton tank (*sic*) was blown over on its side, just from the blast. It was these broadsides from the warships, more than the defensive fighting of the enemy's troops, which halted our division's Panzer Regiment." At all events, after this sharp lesson, the Germans gave up any further idea of throwing the enemy back into the sea.

Montgomery, in his June 30 directive to Generals Bradley and Dempsey, declared himself to be quite satisfied

with the results obtained, although Operation "Epsom" had only dented the enemy line.

"All this is good ... by forcing the enemy to place the bulk of his strength in front of the Second Army, we have made easier the acquisition of territory on the western flank.

"Our policy has been so successful that the Second Army is now opposed by a formidable array of German Panzer Divisions – eight definitely identified, and possibly more to come ...

"To hold the maximum number of enemy divisions on our eastern flank between Caen and Villers Bocage, and to swing the western or right flank of the Army Group southwards and eastwards in a wide sweep so as to threaten the line of withdrawal of such enemy divisions to the south of Paris."

◁ *A "brewed-up" Sherman with the remains of its crew shrouded with a blanket.*
△ *American combat team: rifles, tommy-guns, and a mortar.*

Caen occupied

The carrying out of this plan meant continuing to place the main weight of this battle of attrition on the shoulders of General Dempsey, for the slightest

Just when the American 1st Army was preparing Operation "Cobra", which was to crush German resistance, Montgomery asked Dempsey for one more effort to engage and tie down the Panzers on his front, and, if possible, to advance the armoured units of his 2nd Army into the region around Falaise. To this end, Operation "Goodwood" had moved the centre of gravity of the attack back to the right bank of the Orne, where the British 1st and 8th Armies were massed, whilst the Canadian II Corps, two divisions strong, was concentrated within the ruins of Caen. To it fell the task of capturing the suburbs of the town to the south of the river, and of developing an attack towards Falaise. The enemy's front, tied down in the centre, would be by-passed and rolled back from left to right by the three armoured divisions (the 7th and 11th, and the Guards Armoured Divisions), breaking out from the narrow bridgehead between the Orne and the Dives, which General Gale's parachute troops had captured on the night of June 5-6. In addition to the divisional or brigade tanks, Montgomery had created a reserve of 500 brand-new tanks in Normandy; as for artillery, there were 720 guns of all calibres, and 250,000 shells. But above all, the Allied air forces would support and prepare the attack on a scale hitherto undreamed of: 1,600 four-engined planes, and 600 two-engined planes and fighter-bombers would drop more than 7,000 tons of explosives on enemy positions, and then support VIII Corps' armour as it advanced.

However, the Germans had seen through the Allies' intentions, and had organised themselves to a depth of ten miles; it is true that they only had in the line one division, the 16th Luftwaffe Field Division, and what was left of the 21st Panzer Division, but they still possessed considerable fire-power, in the shape of 272 6-tube rocket launchers and a hundred or so 8.8-cm anti-aircraft guns operating as anti-tank guns.

On July 18, at 0530 hours, the thunder of 720 guns signalled the beginning of Operation "Goodwood". Then, as one member of VIII Corps put it, the aircraft "came lounging across the sky, scattered, leisurely, indifferent. The first ones crossed our lines, and the earth began to shake to a continuous rumble which lasted for three-quarters of an hour; and at no time during that period were fewer than fifty 'planes visible. The

slackening of pressure would mean that Rommel would be able to reorganise and re-form.

On July 9, Caen and Carpiquet aerodrome fell to Lieutenant-General J. T. Crocker's British I Corps. The old Norman town, already badly bombed by the R.A.F. on the night of June 5-6, was now reduced to rubble by the dropping of 2,500 tons of bombs. The only part more or less spared was the area around the majestic Abbaye-aux-Hommes, which was protected by the Geneva Convention and was a refuge for many thousands of homeless. Although this pitiless bombing forced the *"Hitlerjugend"* Division to retreat, it also created such ruin, and slowed down the advance of the Canadian 3rd Division so much, that when it arrived at the river Orne it found all the bridges blown.

din was tremendous. We could see the bombs leaving the 'planes and drifting down almost gently, like milt from a salmon, and as they disappeared behind the trees the rumble rose a little and then sunk to its old level again. The Jocks were all standing grinning at the sky. After weeks of skulking in trenches, here was action; action on a bigger scale than any of them had dreamed was possible."

At 0745 hours the 11th Armoured Division, preceded by a continuous barrage of an intensity never before experienced, began to advance, and quickly got through the first position, defended by troops still groggy from the pounding inflicted by Bomber Command. But towards mid-day the attack came up against the railway line running from Caen to Paris, where it stopped.

This was due, first, to the fact that the British artillery, which had stayed

△ *British Bren-gunner on the Caen–Falaise front, where every ruined house was a nest of resistance by the hard-pressed German forces.*
▷ *An American paratroop patrol encounters German corpses.*
▷▷ *The eternal hedgerows of the Normandy bocage country.*

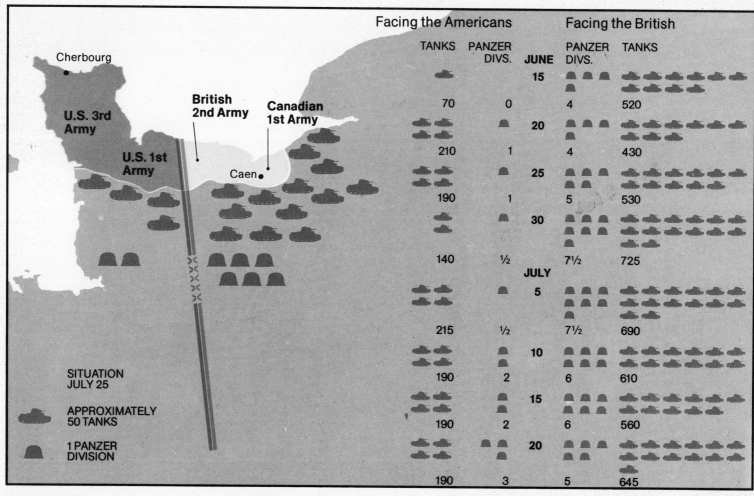

	Facing the Americans			Facing the British	
	TANKS	PANZER DIVS.		PANZER DIVS.	TANKS
JUNE					
15	70	0		4	520
20	210	1		4	430
25	190	1		5	530
30	140	½		7½	725
JULY					
5	215	½		7½	690
10	190	2		6	610
15	190	2		6	560
20	190	3		5	645

Cherbourg

U.S. 3rd Army

U.S. 1st Army

British 2nd Army

Canadian 1st Army

Caen

SITUATION JULY 25

APPROXIMATELY 50 TANKS

1 PANZER DIVISION

on the left bank of the Orne, no longer had the enemy within range; and second, that on the bridges which the Guards and the 7th Armoured Division had to take to get across to the right bank and link up with the 11th Division, there were tremendous bottlenecks. Above all, however, was the fact that 8.8-cm guns and *Nebelwerfers* were firing from the many villages on the outskirts of the town. At nightfall the 1st S.S. Panzer Division *"Leibstandarte"*, which formed Sepp Dietrich's reserve, surprised the 11th Armoured Division, just when it was about to bed down, and according to its commander, Major-General Wisch, destroyed about 40 of its tanks.

Meagre success for the British

On July 19, with the rain taking a hand, the terrain got into such a state owing to the bombing the day before, that operations had to stop. South and south-west of Caen, the British and Canadians had advanced about five miles into the enemy's defensive positions, but had not succeeded in overrunning them. All in all it was rather a meagre success, especially as it had been paid for at the enormous price of 413 tanks, but there was a certain strategic compensation, as the 116th Panzer Division of the German 15th Army, stationed up till then near Amiens, was ordered to move towards Caen; even worse, Kluge, Rommel's successor at the head of *Panzergruppe* "West", fearing a British breakthrough in the direction of Falaise, thought it advisable to move his 2nd Panzer Division from Saint Lô to Caen, less than a week before the beginning of Operation "Cobra".

The British losses relatively small

By this same day of July 19, the losses of the British 2nd Army since June 6 had amounted to 34,700 officers and men, of whom 6,010 were killed, and 28,690 were missing. They were therefore far less severe than those suffered during the same period by the American 1st Army

(62,028 men). Of course, on D-Day the American 1st Division, on "Omaha" Beach, and the 82nd and 101st Airborne Divisions, around Sainte Mère-Eglise, had had a harder time of it. But in the Normandy woodlands the infantry-based American attacks had also been more expensive, in terms of men, than the British tank-based attacks in the Caen area—which seemed to prove once more Guderian's theory that tanks are a weapon that saves lives.

Montgomery's tactics

Basing his calculations on the figures supplied by Brigadier Williams, head of his Intelligence staff, Montgomery saw a situation arising in which, in spite of the apparent failures of the British 2nd Army, he would in a few days be able to send in the American 1st Army. Between June 6 and July 25, the Germans had seen the Allies shift the centre of gravity of their attacks to the south of Caen, as can be seen from the chart at left, based on figures culled from Montgomery's *Memoirs*.

The British A.E.C. Mark III armoured car

Weight: 12.7 tons.
Crew: 4.
Armament: one 75-mm gun and one 7.92-mm Besa machine gun.
Armour: 30-mm maximum.
Engine: one A.E.C. 6-cylinder Diesel, 158-hp.
Speed: 41 mph.
Range: 250 miles.
Length: 18 feet 5 inches.
Width: 8 feet 10½ inches.
Height: 8 feet 10 inches.

The American Chevrolet T17E1 Staghound I armoured car

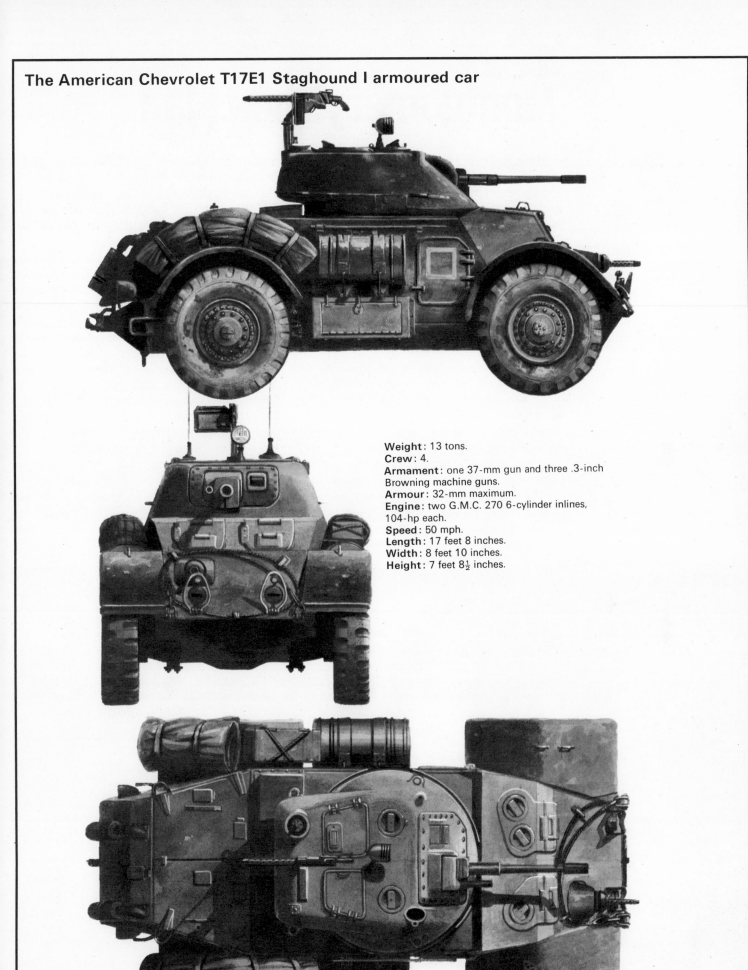

Weight: 13 tons.
Crew: 4.
Armament: one 37-mm gun and three .3-inch Browning machine guns.
Armour: 32-mm maximum.
Engine: two G.M.C. 270 6-cylinder inlines, 104-hp each.
Speed: 50 mph.
Length: 17 feet 8 inches.
Width: 8 feet 10 inches.
Height: 7 feet $8\frac{1}{2}$ inches.

CHAPTER 121

Montgomery's new plan

Although, of course, Montgomery's superiors, General Eisenhower and the Combined Chiefs-of-Staff Committee, as well as his most important subordinates, were aware of the strategic objective hidden by his apparently slow manoeuvres, S.H.A.E.F. was beginning to show some signs of impatience. Writing ten years after the event, Montgomery thought he saw personal reasons, unconnected with the military situation, behind many of the criticisms made of his methods within the Allied High Command.

"One of the reasons for this in my belief was that the original COSSAC plan had been, in fact, to break out from the Caen–Falaise area, on our eastern flank. I had refused to accept this plan and had changed it. General Morgan who had made the COSSAC plan was now at Supreme Headquarters as Deputy Chief of Staff. He considered Eisenhower was a god; since I had discarded many of his plans, he placed me at the other end of the celestial ladder. So here were the

seeds of discord. Morgan and those around him (the displaced strategists) lost no opportunity of trying to persuade Eisenhower that I was defensively minded and that we were unlikely to break out anywhere!"

As far as Sir Frederick Morgan is concerned, Montgomery may have been right, but he is surely on more dangerous ground when he goes on to assert that Air-Marshal Coningham, commander of the Tactical Air Force, associated himself with these criticisms for similar reasons. "Coningham", he wrote, "was particularly interested in getting his airfields south-west of Caen. They were mentioned in the plan and to him they were all-important. I don't blame him. But they were not all-important to me. If we won the battle of Normandy, everything else would follow, airfields and all. I wasn't fighting to capture airfields; I was fighting to defeat Rommel in Normandy. This Coningham could scarcely appreciate: and for two reasons. First, we were not seeing each

▽ *American sappers probe for mines on one of the approach-roads to St. Lô. The wreckage of a jeep trailer, recent victims of a mine, litters the ditch to the left.*
▷▷ *False alarm. A Frenchman nervously "surrenders" to a bespectacled American rifleman.*

other daily as in the desert days, for at this stage I was working direct to Leigh-Mallory. Secondly, Coningham wanted the airfields in order to defeat Rommel, whereas I wanted to defeat Rommel in order, only incidentally, to capture the airfields.''

And events were to show that in order to defeat Army Group ''B'', it was unnecessary to be in possession of the airfields that Coningham would have liked. It is still true, however, that by remaining in the Caen area, instead of wearing the enemy down in the Falaise area, 15 miles further south, as the original project had planned, the British 2nd Army asked its air force for a great deal of support, and yet placed it in a difficult position.

In the Normandy beach-head airfields were scarce, and their runways were so short that for the pilots getting fighter-bombers loaded with a ton of bombs or rockets into the air was a real problem. And landing posed similar problems; as Belfield and Essame have noted, ''anyone who flew over the bridgehead in Normandy must have retained vivid memories of fighter aircraft, twin engined Dakotas (used as ambulances) and the small Austers all milling about in a horribly confined airspace. The perpetual risk of collisions greatly increased the strain on the pilots who had to fly from the bridgehead''.

It may be that the commander of the 2nd Tactical Air Force did not like being treated as a subordinate by the man with whom he had been on equal terms in North Africa, but his criticisms did not all spring from personal ill-feeling. And it should be noted that at S.H.A.E.F. Air-Marshals Leigh-Mallory and Tedder both approved Coningham's attitude.

As for Eisenhower, it may fairly be said that his memoirs are marked with a calm philosophy that he was far from feeling when Operation ''Goodwood'' was breaking down on the Bourguébus ridge. For after all, according to the plan worked out by Montgomery, Bradley's enveloping movement ought to have begun on D-Day plus seventeen, June 23, when the Allies would be firmly established on a front extending from Granville to Caen, passing through Vire, Argentan, and Falaise. ''This meant'', he wrote, ''that Falaise would be in our possession before the great wheel began. The line that we actually held when the breakout began on D plus 50 was approximately that planned for D plus 5.

"This was a far different story, but one which had to be accepted. Battle is not a one-sided affair. It is a case of action and reciprocal action repeated over and over again as contestants seek to gain position and other advantage by which they may inflict the greatest possible damage upon their respective opponents."

Be that as it may, in his opinion Montgomery needed a touch not of the brake, but of the accelerator, and Eisenhower's repeated efforts to get Montgomery to show more aggression could not have failed to annoy his troublesome subordinate.

In this argument, which went as far as Winston Churchill, Montgomery had a faithful defender in Brooke, who did all he could to prevent this potential conflict from becoming too bitter. At the time Montgomery was also on the best of terms with Bradley, who wrote that "Montgomery exercised his Allied authority with wisdom, forbearance, and restraint. While coordinating our movements with those of Dempsey's Monty carefully avoided getting mixed up in U.S. command decisions, but instead granted us the latitude to operate as freely and as independently as we chose. At no time did he probe into First Army with the indulgent manner he sometimes displayed among those subordinates who were also his countrymen. I could not have wanted a more tolerant or judicious commander. Not once did he confront us with an arbitrary directive and not once did he reject any plan that we had devised."

There is no doubt therefore that Bradley, who enjoyed Eisenhower's full confidence, tried to influence him the same way as Brooke. The differences over strategy that arose between Bradley and Montgomery from the autumn of 1944, and the coolness that affected their relations afterwards, right up to the end of the war, are very well known, which makes Bradley's comments on Montgomery's handling of this initial phase of the Battle of Normandy all the more valuable. "Whilst Collins was hoisting the flag of VII Corps above Cherbourg, Montgomery was losing his reputation in the long and arduous siege of the old university town of Caen. For three weeks he had been engaging his troops against those armoured divisions that he had deliberately lured towards Caen, in accordance with our diversionary strategy. The town was an important communications centre which he would eventually

need, but for the moment the taking of the town was an end in itself, for his task, first and foremost, was to commit German troops against the British front, so that we could capture Cherbourg that much easier, and prepare a further attack.

"In this diversionary mission Monty was more than successful, for the harder he hammered toward Caen, the more German troops he drew into that sector. Too many correspondents, however, had overrated the importance of Caen itself, and when Monty failed to take it, they

◁ ◁ △ *Montgomery and Bradley confer with Patton, whose 3rd Army would spearhead the breakout operation.*
◁ ◁ ▽ *"Better roll up your map, Herr General – I don't think your counter-attack's going to come off" – a sardonic comment by Giles of the* Daily Express.
△ *Eisenhower takes a snack lunch while visiting the U.S. 79th Division.*

▽ *De Gaulle makes a point to Eisenhower.*

△ *A picture vividly expressive of the strain of the fighting for St. Lô.*

blamed him for the delay. But had we attempted to exonerate Montgomery by explaining how successfully he had hoodwinked the German by diverting him toward Caen from Cotentin, we would have also given our strategy away. We desperately wanted the Germans to believe this attack on Caen was the main Allied effort." It seems pretty clear that Montgomery was right. During World War I, Joffre had been severely criticised for his phrase "I'm nibbling away at them". Thirty years later, it must be admitted that Montgomery, though paying a heavy price, "nibbled" his opponent's armoured units, which were technically superior and on the whole very well trained, to excellent effect.

Caen may thus be compared with Verdun, in World War I, where Colonel-General Falkenhayn intended to bleed the French Army white. But where

the head of the Kaiser's General Staff failed against Joffre, Montgomery succeeded against Rommel, and with the American 1st Army and Patton behind Bradley, he had at his disposal a force ready to exploit the situation such as Falkenhayn never had.

At all events, the accredited pressmen at S.H.A.E.F. did not spare Montgomery, and above him Eisenhower, whom they criticised for tolerating the inefficiency of his second-in-command. It was even insinuated in the American press that with typical British cunning, Montgomery was trying to save his troops at the expense of the Americans, and that, most careful of English lives, he preferred to expend American soldiers, without the naïve Eisenhower realising what was happening.

However far-fetched such quarrels may seem, they continued long after the war, but under a different guise. For after the brilliant success of Operation "Cobra", which took Bradley almost in one fell swoop from Avranches, in Normandy, to Commercy and Maastricht on the Meuse, it would have been both indecent and ridiculous to accuse Montgomery of having kept the best things for the Anglo-Canadian troops, and given the Americans nothing but the scraps. Critics now tried to show that his attempts to tie down the enemy's mobile reserves with General Dempsey's troops failed. Thus, in 1946, Ralph Ingersoll, a war correspondent with Bradley's forces, portrayed the "Master" as being impatient to fight it out with Rommel: "The blow . . . could be struck with British forces under a British headquarters, for British credit and prestige". This would have confirmed Montgomery's domination of the American armies. "The result of Montgomery's decision was the battle of Caen—which was really two battles, two successive all-out attacks, continuing after Caen itself had fallen. Beginning in mid-June and ending nearly a month later, it was a defeat from which British arms on the continent never recovered. It was the first and last all-British battle fought in Europe. As he had feared, Montgomery was never again able to fight alone but thereafter had always to borrow troops and supplies to gain the superiority without which he would not even plan an attack."

What does this mean? That the 2nd British Army's attacks did not reach their geographical objectives is beyond question, but when one realises the tactical and material advantages gained over the enemy, it is impossible to join with Ingersoll and talk of "defeat". This can be seen in the cries of alarm, and later of despair, which German O.B. West sent to O.K.W. Of course, Ingersoll wrote his book in 1946, and was not in a position to appreciate all this.

Hitler's blindness

Colonel-General Count von Schlieffen, the old Chief-of-Staff of the Imperial German Army, used to say to his students at the Military Academy, that when analysing a campaign, due allowance was never given to the way in which the vanquished positively helped the victor. It will therefore be instructive to see how Rommel,

◁ *Once the Germans built dummy tanks to conceal their strength; now the dummies were desperately offered to the swarming Allied fighter-bombers.*
▽ *and* ▽ ▽ *Two typical scenes from the tank battles of July.*

Rundstedt, and Hitler smoothed the path of Montgomery and Eisenhower.

In all this Rundstedt played a very secondary rôle. The great strategist whose Army Group "A" had conquered Poland, and who had played such a big part in the 1940 defeat of France, was as far-sighted as ever. But he no longer dominated, nor did he seem to want to do so; Lieutenant-General Speidel, Chief-of-Staff of Army Group "B", paints him as having adopted an attitude of "sarcastic resignation", considering the "representations" and "despatches full of gravity" sent to Hitler as being the height of wisdom. He did, however, loyally support Rommel in his discussions with Hitler—nothing more, nothing less.

Responsibility for the German defeat in the West therefore has to be shared between Rommel and Hitler. On D-Day, both wondered if this attack was not rather a diversion, covering a second

◁ and △ This was St. Lô. The Americans finally cleared the town on July 18.

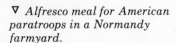

△ *Two nuns and a housewife give directions to a party of G.I.s.*
▷ ▷ *Searchlights and muzzle-flashes make a colourful display at an American A.A. battery.*

▽ *Alfresco meal for American paratroops in a Normandy farmyard.*

landing aimed at the Pas-de-Calais. And against all reason, Hitler stuck to this idea until the end of July, whilst Rommel abandoned it when the American VII Corps' orders fell into his hands. The results of such blindness were catastrophic. To stop the Allies on the front they had reached by June 12, it would have been necessary to disengage the armoured units that Rommel had thrown in against Montgomery in the Caen sector, but this would only have been possible by drawing upon the 15th Army, stationed between the Seine and the Escaut, and the best placed to intervene.

But Hitler expressly forbade Army Group "B" to do this. The Germans were therefore obliged, after scouring Brittany, to seek reinforcements at the very opposite end of France, and on June 12, the 276th Division received orders to leave Bayonne and get to the front: "The broken railways, the destroyed bridges and the French Maquis so delayed them that the last elements of the division finally arrived at Hottot in Normandy on July 4. In other words, to make a journey of some 400 miles, which could normally be completed by rail in seventy-two hours, required no less than twenty-two days. The main body of the division had to march at least one-third of the distance on foot, averaging approximately twenty miles each night."

Similar misfortunes befell the 272nd Division, drawn from Perpignan, and the 274th Division, hastily organised in the Narbonne area; whilst, in order to reach the Caen sector, the 16th L.F.D., on watch over the coast at IJmuiden, had first to follow the Rhine as far as Koblenz. All this makes it easy to understand why Army Group "B" was confined to a series of piecemeal tactical operations, devoid of any overall strategy.

Furthermore, Hitler refused to ratify the arrangements that Rommel had shown him on June 12, preparing to move the bulk of his troops from Caen to the Carentan–Montebourg region, which would to some extent have thwarted the 7th American Army's move against Cherbourg. Hypnotised by the name "Falaise", Hitler played into Montgomery's hands.

Meeting at Soissons

The situation was obviously bound to deteriorate. Therefore Hitler ordered Rommel and Rundstedt to meet him at the command post he had installed in 1940, at Margival, near Soissons, when Operation *"Seelöwe"* had been planned to conquer Great Britain. According to Lieutenant-General Speidel's account: "Hitler had arrived with Colonel-General Jodl and staff on the morning of June 17. He had travelled in an armoured car from Metz, where he had flown from Berchtesgaden. He looked pale and worn for lack of sleep. His fingers played nervously with his spectacles and the pencils before him. Hunched on a stool, with his marshals standing before him,

△ *Captured while he slept, a German soldier hurriedly hauls on his boots under the gaze of his captor.*

▽ *Objective Falaise–a Canadian column on the move.*

his former magnetism seemed to have vanished.

"After a few cold words of greeting, Hitler, in a high, bitter voice, railed on about the success of the Allied landing, and tried to blame the local commanders. He ordered that Cherbourg be held at all costs."

Rommel, who also spoke for Rundstedt, defended his officers from these attacks. When they began to discuss future action, the gulf between the two commanders and their garrulous leader became even more pronounced.

In Hitler's view, the use of flying bombs would soon bring the Third Reich victory, provided that they were concentrated against London; whereas, logically, it was suggested that he ought to use them against the embarkation ports which were sending over reinforcements to Normandy. Hitler did not deny the shortcomings of the Luftwaffe, but asserted that within a short time the coming into service of jet fighters would wrest from the Allies their present supremacy, and thus allow the Wehrmacht's land forces to resume the initiative. But without Hitler's earlier intervention, the jets would have already entered service ...

Hitler intervenes ...

Above all, however, was the fact that Rommel, backed by Rundstedt, categorically rejected the possibility of a second Allied landing north of the Seine, and demanded complete freedom of action, for it was now to be expected that the enemy would "break out of the Caen and Bayeux areas, and also from the Cotentin, towards the south, aiming for Paris, with a secondary attack upon Avranches to isolate Brittany". To cancel out this threat, they would have to bring into action the infantry divisions stationed in the Orne sector, then carry out "a limited withdrawal to be made southwards, with the object of launching an armoured thrust into the flank of the enemy and fighting the battle outside the range of the enemy's naval artillery ..."

Hitler vetoed this plan absolutely: it was to be total resistance, no retreat, as at the time of the Battle of Moscow. Events have shown that this policy condemned the German forces in Normandy to disaster. But whether Rommel's plan would have been possible, given the

enormous Allied superiority and the delapidated state of his troops, is doubtful, to say the least.

. . . and changes the High Command

As was to be expected, the fall of Cherbourg and the Cotentin operations increased even further the tension between those at the front and Hitler.

Furious at the way things were going, the Führer, despite Rommel's and Rundstedt's objections, ordered Colonel-General Dollman to be the subject of a judicial enquiry. On hearing this news, Dollman suffered a heart attack at Le Mans on June 29, and was replaced at the head of the 7th Army by General Hausser, who handed over command of II *Waffen*-S.S. Panzer Corps to his colleague Bittrich. On the same day *Panzergruppe* "West" was re-christened the 5th *Panzerarmee,* but General Geyr von Schweppenburg, only just recovered from the wounds he had sustained on June 12, having resumed command, had been dismissed and

replaced by General Eberbach, because he had had the temerity to point out the strategic patching-up of the Supreme Command.

The same day also, Rommel and Rundstedt were called to the Berghof by Hitler, who, however, refused to speak to them in private, and added nothing new to the rantings with which he had assailed their ears at Margival, about the decisive effect which the new weapons would have upon the course of the war. As for the two marshals, they emphasised the urgent necessity of ending the war on the west, so as to enable the Reich to fight on in the east. On seeing the indignant way in which their suggestion was greeted, they both thought they were going to be sacked on the spot. In fact the Führer's wrath fell only on Rundstedt, and even then it was somewhat mitigated by the award of the Oak Leaves to his Knight's Cross. He was replaced by Kluge, who had now recovered from the winter car accident which had obliged him to give up his command on the Eastern Front. At the Berghof, the new Supreme Commander in the West was duly spoken to by Hitler, Keitel, and Jodl, who impressed upon him the necessity of making his subordinate, Rommel, see reason. Hence the violent incident which took place at la Roche-Guyon, when the hero of Tobruk was told in no uncertain terms by his new chief that "he would now have to get accustomed to carrying out orders".

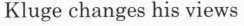

Kluge changes his views

Rommel reacted to these remarks with a written protest on July 3, to which he added a long aide-mémoire in justification, whose reasoning, both honest and full of good sense, led Kluge, an intelligent man, completely to revise his opinion.

In any case, the developing situation in Normandy allowed no other conclusion than Rommel's. The 5th *Panzerarmee* and the 7th Army were still containing the Allied advance, but with more and more difficulty. Despite their losses, Allied numbers and supplies were increasing daily, whereas the German forces' losses could not be made up. Between June 6 and July 15 it had only received 6,000 men to replace 97,000 killed, missing, and wounded, amongst whom there were 2,360 officers, including 28 generals and 354 lieutenant-generals. And its sup-

△ *Moment of humour during Churchill's visit to the beach-head: a Cherbourg worker offers the Prime Minister a light.*

△ *A drink of water and a cigarette for a wounded German.*

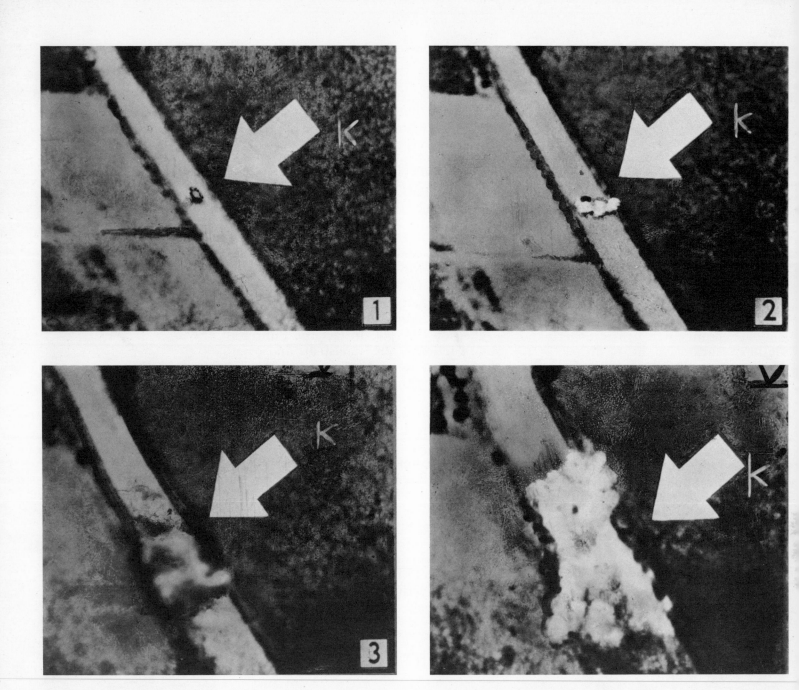

△ *Was this the attack that knocked Rommel out of the battle for Normandy? These pictures are "stills" from the camera-gun film exposed during a strafing run by Lieutenant Harold O. Miller of the U.S. 8th Air Force. For a while it was believed that Rommel had been killed in the attack–but he survived. There was a grimmer fate in store for him . . .*

ply position had become so precarious because of enemy bombing that the most drastic economies were imposed.

Such were the facts that Rommel, with the approval of Kluge, pointed out in his last report to Hitler on July 15 1944–a sad catalogue leading to the following conclusions:

"It must therefore be expected that within the next two to three weeks, the enemy will break through our weakened front, and advance in depth through France, an action which will have the gravest consequences.

"Everywhere our troops are fighting heroically, but this unequal struggle is inevitably drawing to a close. I am forced to ask you to draw the necessary conclusions from this situation, without delay. As leader of your Western forces,

I felt it my duty to explain it to you as clearly as possible."

What would have happened if Rommel had not been badly wounded on the Livarot–Vimoutiers road, the very day after dispatching this strong message? Hitler would almost certainly have refused, told him that he must not surrender, and would probably even have dismissed him. In that event, would Rommel have sent officers to parley with Montgomery? He would have been able to count on all his general staff, and certain field-commanders, such as Lüttwitz and Schwerin, at the head of the 2nd and 116th Panzer Divisions respectively. But would he have taken this enormous step when the shattering news came through of the bomb attempt on Hitler's life and the collapse of the "July Plot"?

CHAPTER 122
The July Plot

by Jacques Nobécourt

1710

On April 7, 1943, Lieutenant-Colonel Claus von Stauffenberg, head of the Operations Staff of the 10th Panzer Division, was severely wounded by a strafing American aircraft while his unit was withdrawing in southern Tunisia. He lost his right hand, two fingers of his left hand, and his left eye. In August, when barely recovered from his wounds, he was appointed to the General Staff of the Reserve Army in Berlin; and there he began to make contact with the leaders of the anti-Hitler movement.

On July 20, 1944, Stauffenberg placed within a few feet of Hitler a bomb which should not have failed to kill him, and afterwards flew back to the offices of the War Ministry in Berlin, where he tried in vain to organise a takeover of power by the Wehrmacht. That night, under the glare of truck headlights, he was shot with three other officers. General Beck, former Chief of the Army General Staff and figurehead of the resistance movement in the Army, had committed suicide shortly before. Beck was 64 years old, Stauffenberg 38. They represented two generations of German officers—two totally different men, both symbolising the dilemma of an army powerless in the face of a doctrinaire dictatorship which was dragging its country to ruin.

These dramatic scenes did not have their origin in the war; for that one must go back some ten years. The basic conflict which resulted in the "July Plot" –the National Socialist conception of the state versus the opposition elements summed up by the phrase "German resistance"–had its roots in the conditions behind Hitler's accession to power on January 30, 1933. This event had been greeted with cautious relief by the small officer corps of the professional Army. Party anarchy ceased. Order returned to the streets. Social measures put an end to strikes and unemployment. And the new Chancellor pledged himself to the full restoration of Germany's national honour. More than any other man, Hitler seemed capable of "breaking the shackles of Versailles" at last.

Under the official aegis of the elderly Field-Marshal von Hindenburg, President of the Republic, Hitler's régime seemed to be a satisfactory compromise. Sponsored by leading conservatives, it was supported by tightly-controlled militants. It appeared to stand halfway between the Imperial monarchy which still inspired nostalgia in many soldiers, and the Republic which they served without genuine enthusiasm. Hitler, after all, had given every assurance that the constitution of the armed forces would ensure the restoration of Germany's political power. But what was to come next? The conquest of new *Lebensraum* in the East. But when this was put to the Army and Navy commanders on February 3, 1933, the programme caused deep mistrust–particularly in officers such as Lieutenant-Colonel Fromm, who were to find themselves confronted with Stauffenberg on July 20, 1944. But no active opposition ensued.

◁ ◁ *Adolf Hitler, Führer and Reich Chancellor, in 1938, the year of his greatest bloodless victories: the Austrian Anschluss and the takeover of the Czech Sudetenland. He had become head of state by constitutional methods and had led Germany to unheard-of triumphs. And even by 1944, with disaster closing in on the Reich from east and west, his hold over the German nation was as firm as ever.*

▽ *This view of Hitler's triumphal visit to Memel in 1939 shows the three main planks of his power: well-drilled Party officials, rapturous civilians –and the troops of the Wermacht, every man of them bound to the Führer by oath.*

DIE WEHRMACHT

AUSGABE A
Berlin, 3 März 1943
7. Jahrgang Nr. 5
Belg. 2 Fr., Bulg. 8 Lewa, Dänemark 40 Öre, Finnl. 4,50 mk.,
Frankr. 4 Fr., Griechenl. 30 Dr.,
Ital. 2 Lire, Kroatien 5 Kuna,
Niederld. 20 Cts., Norwegen
40 Öre, Portugal 2.— Esc.,
Rumän. 20 Lei, Serb. 4 Dinar,
Spanien 1,25 Pts., Schweden
45 Öre, Schweiz 40 Rappen,
Slowakei 2,50 Ks., Türkei
12,50 Kurus, Ungarn 36 fillér.

HERAUSGEGEBEN VOM OBERKOMMANDO DER WEHRMACHT

Changing conditions

While Hindenburg was still alive, the German officer corps followed his lead and did not bother itself too much with the doings of the Nazi régime. But Hindenburg's death changed all that. The young Colonel Guderian—still, at the time, dreaming of impossible armoured divisions—was moved to write the following lines to his wife when he heard of the old Field-Marshal's death on August 1, 1934:

"The old gentleman is no more. We are all saddened by this irreplaceable loss. He was like a father to the whole nation and particularly to the armed forces, and it will be a long and hard time before the great gap that he leaves in our national life can be filled. His existence alone meant more to foreign powers than any numbers of written agreements and fine words. He possessed the confidence of the world. We, who loved and honoured him, have become much poorer for his death. Tomorrow we swear the oath to Hitler. An oath heavy with consequences. Pray God that both sides may abide by it equally for the welfare of Germany. The Army is accustomed to keep its oaths. May the Army be able, in honour, to do so this time."

On August 2 not a single German officer refused to take the oath which bound him explicitly to the person of Adolf Hitler. But all the questions raised by the oath, all the worries which it created, even the diversity of meanings in "the welfare of

Germany", can be read between the lines of Guderian's letter.

The Army stood apart from the liquidation of all political opposition, not lifting a finger to stop the Socialist, Catholic, and Communist leaders from being thrown into concentration camps. Its policy of benevolent neutrality was confirmed by the plebiscite of August 19, 1934. It was reassured by the subsequent liquidation of Röhm and the right wing of the Nazi Party. But all too soon the Army found itself on the defensive. In its rôle as an instrument of foreign policy the Army understood that that policy must be reasonable, suited to military resources, and vaguely based on the idea of German

◁ ◁ *Cover of* Wehrmacht *at the time of Stalingrad, idolising the heroism of the troops at the front.*

△ *and* ▽ *On the eve of war, Hitler visits the Siegfried Line. The general on the left of the Führer in both pictures is Erwin von Witzleben, commanding in the West in 1939—and a key conspirator by 1944.*

Col. von Stauffenberg

THE K

Gen. Olbricht

Gen. Tresckow

Gen. Beck

F. M. von Kluge

Col. Mertz von Quirnheim

F. M. von Witzleben

Gen. von Stülpnagel

Col. von Haeften

Gen. Hoeppner

Adm. Canaris

Gen. Oster

1714

CONSPIRATORS

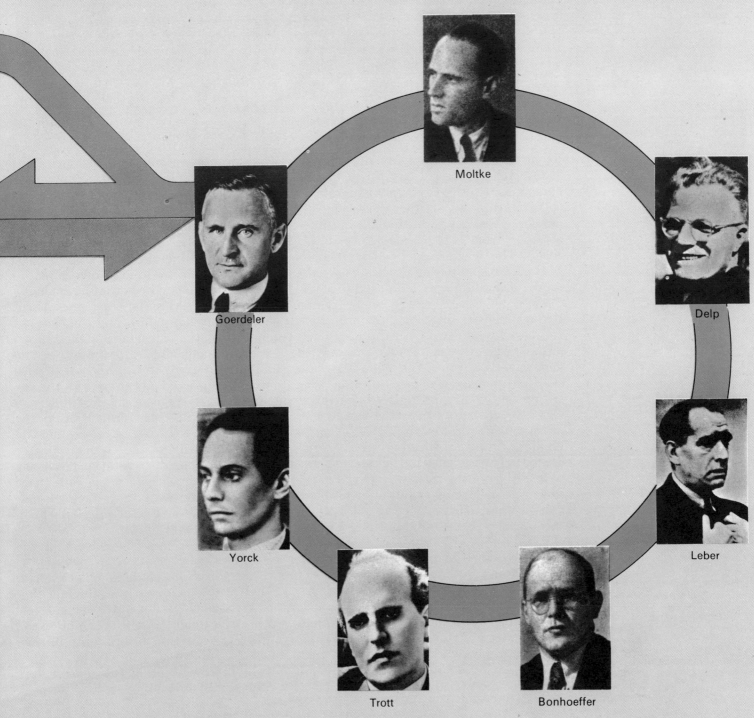

Moltke

Delp

Goerdeler

Yorck

Leber

Trott

Bonhoeffer

This chart shows the inter-relation of the leading members of the German resistance and the men they hoped to involve. At bottom left are Canaris and Oster, the conspirators of the Abwehr or German Military Intelligence; General Beck and Field-Marshal von Witzleben, together with ex-Panzer General Hoeppner, form the right-hand column. To their left are Olbricht, Haeften, and Mertz von Quirnheim from Reserve Army H.Q. in Berlin's Bendlerstrasse, and General von Tresckow, who made repeated efforts to organise attempts on Hitler's life from Army Group "Centre" in Russia. General von Stülpnagel, Military Governor of France, was to direct operations from Paris once the news of Hitler's death came in. Finally there is the elusive figure of Field-Marshal von Kluge, who refused to act in the few brief hours when the conspiracy could have succeeded, and committed suicide afterwards. The civilian conspirators at right included Carl Goerdeler, former Mayor of Leipzig; the courageous priests Bonhoeffer and Delp; the Socialist Julius Leber–all members of Count von Moltke's "Kreisau Circle". This was a resistance group of young idealists formed before the war, which included Adam von Trott zu Solz and Count Peter Yorck von Wartenburg.

sovereignty. But none of the Army leaders of the time saw the real, long-term explosive power of ideology backed by totalitarian power.

This failure to face the facts characterised the members of the German resistance movement until late into the war. Their sincere nationalism lacked the one thing which would have given them victory in the civil war which they were prepared to risk: ruthless fanaticism.

Caution the watchword

From the official birthday of the new Wehrmacht on May 16, 1935, to the French campaign of 1940, the Army generals, in their relations with Hitler, were primarily concerned with preventing the military machine from being used before it was ready. The vast majority of Germany's ranking officers buried themselves in the work of building up a national army. Shaken by the excessive tempo which Hitler imposed on them, the top commanders laid it down that the Reich was still too weak to risk a head-on clash with a hostile coalition. The generals were still haunted by memories of 1918. But Hitler, taking the gamble, overcame them. The only man to sense that the Rhineland venture of March 7, 1936, was a viable one, he went ahead. And on November 5, 1937 he revealed his long-term plans to the Wehrmacht commanders: "It is my irrevocable decision to settle the problem of German living-space by 1943-45 at the latest." If, before this time, France suffered an internal crisis or went to war with Italy, the Reich could seize Czechoslovakia and Austria with impunity.

Here, clearly revealed, was Hitler's programme. And General Beck, shocked and driven by the need to settle the pangs of conscience which had bedevilled him since taking the oath to Hitler in August 1934 (when he had toyed with the idea of resigning), stood out in opposition to Hitler's policy.

Born in 1880 and a general staff officer since 1911, Ludwig Beck had built up his prestige by qualities which were more those of an intellectual than of a soldier. He was the complete opposite of the traditional idea of a soldier or even of a military commander, but his intelligence, his insight, and his shrewdness impressed themselves on all who came in contact with him.

But his later career revealed the reverse sides of these fine qualities. He was too much of an analyst to back daring or risky moves. He was too meticulous to go ahead without having first amassed all the information and covered all possibilities. He saw things too clearly to be able to cope with the consequences of a setback. In all these ways Beck was very similar to his opposite number, General Gamelin, whom he met during a trip to Paris in 1937. "Significant of his way of thinking was his much-vaunted method of fighting which he called 'delaying defence'," noted Guderian.

Was it likely that such a dyed-in-the-wool procrastinator and arch-priest of caution could have headed a conspiracy or an opposition movement? The fact remains that Beck was the only general to risk his career and reputation by so doing. Yet his revolt was motivated more than by anything else by his philosophy of the rôle of the German officer in the state. It was said of Beck that he made the German land forces the brain and instrument of German policy, and the German general staff the "conscience of the Army". German commanders should define limited situations in the light of precise data and proceed according to the resources at their disposal. Nothing was more alien to this idea of Beck's than the Nazi myth of race and of blood, and the notion of spreading the German master race through the great land spaces of the East. Beck, however, ruled out these ideas on account of their lack of proportion and balance before he condemned them on ethical grounds.

Right to the end, the officers of the anti-Hitler movement were inspired by the image of the German officer corps. "Their ideology stems from the fact that the Wehrmacht is an autonomous body within the Reich, an entity which exists in its own right and according to its own laws," commented one of the reports on the interrogation of the conspirators in the plot of July 20.

More power for Hitler

After Hitler's address on November 5, 1937, Beck countered by urging his own commander, Fritsch, to warn Hitler to confine himself to possibilities and not to be side-tracked by desirabilities. Beck's uneasiness mirrored that felt by other

Army commanders; but once again Hitler reacted too fast for the Army. He assessed the internal divisions of the general staff. He took into account the natural rivalry between the generations in the officer corps. He estimated that the national character of the armed forces, swelled as they were by compulsory service, would cancel out the resistance of the "Prussian technocrats". Step by step Hitler eliminated the War Minister, Field-Marshal von Blomberg – although the latter opposed the malcontents of the Army – and General von Fritsch, Commander-in-Chief of the Army. And on February 4, 1938 Hitler became Commander-in-Chief of the Wehrmacht. Promotions and postings advanced many generals who would make their names in the war.

Retained as Chief-of-Staff of the Army, command of which went to General von Brauchitsch, Beck refused to modify his opinions. Hitler said of him at this time, speaking to his Minister of Justice: "Beck is the only man I fear. That man would be able to undertake anything against me." Moreover, Beck remained in contact with several leading personalities who did not conceal their hostility to the régime – Admiral Canaris, chief of the *Abwehr,* German counter-espionage; Carl Goerdeler, former mayor of Leipzig, who contributed much confused activity to the embryo opposition move-

ment; and the diplomat Ulrich von Hassel, German Ambassador at Rome.

Without doubt this was basically nothing more than a loose net of malcontents with neither leaders nor programme. Hitler had just added still more to his powers by bringing the Army under his sway. And yet it was in this spring of 1938 that Beck began to add to the conspiracy the following officers whom he deemed reliable: Colonel Hans Oster, A.D.C. to Canaris in the *Abwehr*; Generals Erwin von Witzleben, Erich Hoeppner, Karl-Heinrich von Stülpnagel, Eduard Wagner, Franz Halder, and Kurt von Hammerstein-Equord. The civilians included the magistrates Hans von Dohnanyi and Justus Delbrück, Pastor Dietrich Bonhoeffer, and the land-owner Carl Ludwig von Guttenberg.

These formed the hard core, and nearly all of them died after July 20, 1944. Some of their stories make sad telling. Too many of them continued to serve the régime they were attempting to overthrow. Oster, for example, had pushed his personal convictions into the realms of high treason by warning Norway and Holland of the date of the imminent German attacks. (He hoped in so doing to force the victims to react in time and shorten the war.) But Witzleben and Hoeppner commanded in France and Russia until the end of 1941. In 1942 Stülpnagel became Military Governor of France, and his record

▽ *Claus Schenk von Stauffenberg, the "iron man" of the conspiracy, whose will led to the attempt on July 20. He is seen here earlier in his career as a young cavalry officer.*
▽▽ *Stauffenberg, still recovering from the severe wounds he suffered in Tunisia, seen with his children.*

there was so forbidding that it was not cancelled out by his rôle in the July Plot, followed though this was by his abortive suicide attempt on the battlefield of Verdun. Halder, who succeeded Beck as Army Chief-of-Staff, and Wagner, Army Quartermaster-General, worked simultaneously on their plans for an Army *coup* and on the technical details of the offensives in the West and in Russia.

In the summer of 1938, General Hoeppner commanded the new 1st Light Division at Wuppertal. (The 1st Light was redesignated 6th Panzer Division on the outbreak of war.) At this time he had posted to his staff as head of the logistic services (Department 1b) the young Captain von Stauffenberg, fresh from the War Academy. It was to be many years before their destinies combined. In 1938 Hoeppner would certainly not have sympathised with the deep-rooted opinions of his new staff officer. But Stauffenberg himself was like other officers of his own generation. They felt themselves to be men apart, as technicians of the military arm, and certainly not as rebels. "Certainly, we tended to criticise heavily

certain aspects of the Party in our daily talk," one of Stauffenberg's colleagues was to say. "But I would not pretend for one moment that Stauffenberg showed any opposition to Hitler or to the Party. For Stauffenberg as for ourselves, Hitler was the Reich Chancellor, and it was to Hitler that we had sworn allegiance on the flag."

Beck resigns

Beck's renewed warnings on May 5 and July 16, 1938, stressed his belief that to follow such a policy could only result in a prolonged global war. He argued to Brauchitsch that the Army leaders should resign *en bloc* and shoulder "their responsibility towards the majority of their people", for, as he added, "exceptional times demand exceptional measures". But the young officers remained deaf to Beck's arguments.

By advocating "exceptional measures" Beck was on the verge of preaching a *coup d'état*, to be carried out in legal

fashion, which would add power to a strike by the generals. He put his cards on the table to Brauchitsch: he wanted not only to avoid war, but to restore "normal judicial conditions" by smashing the Party and the S.S. by force.

"Let there be no doubt that our actions are not directed against Hitler but against the evil gang which is leading him to ruin . . . nothing we do should give the impression of a plot. It is also essential that all the generals support us and support us to the end, whatever the consequences . . . Our watchwords must be brief and clear: for the Führer – against war – against the Party favourites – freedom of expression – the end of police-state methods – restoration of justice in the Reich – Prussian decency and simplicity."

But the generals did not offer their support. Hitler secured their obedience. And Beck offered his resignation, which was accepted. He retired on September 1, becoming a passive and increasingly impatient spectator of a chain of events which he had forecast long before – but without defining any practical short-term remedies.

One unequivocal belief motivated Beck: "A soldier's duty of obedience ends as soon as he is given an order which is incompatible with his conscience, his knowledge, and his sense of responsibility." As the war progressed the stakes involved would be increased more and more, in such a way as to make the problem vital for those who remained loyal until the last possible minute. To have laid this principle down so precisely as early as 1938 was to Beck's credit. From 1938 his activity in the anti-Nazi field continued to develop and to grow more heated – but without becoming any more organised or disciplined, and he was always putting off the decision until a favourable moment should arrive.

It is, therefore, obvious that the story of the German resistance had deep roots. The outbreak of war in 1939 was only a minor milestone, and the development of the war had only partial effects on the real problem. The basic issues at stake were already established: the restlessness of the long tradition of the "military state" and its relations with the sovereign power, a tradition which was founded as much on genuine values as on political expediency.

"In ridding Germany of Hitler, the generals seem to be looking to the Führer for orders," noted Hassel in his diary. Sarcastic, certainly, but not without truth. The fact that the head of state was also Hitler, the trouble-maker, troubled many a conscience. Forcible resistance would lead Germany to civil war and expose the Reich to the same "stab in the back" which, according to Hindenburg, the "civilians" of 1918 had dealt the Imperial Army. And what would resistance achieve, in concrete terms? Better, surely, to end the war with an honourable peace, which would leave the fruits of victory secure. The problem of doing away with a régime which was dishonouring Germany remained unresolved until as late as 1943.

First stirrings of active resistance

The different streams of resistance at the same time chimed in with movements which were as organised as could be, given the need for secrecy, in the occupied countries. The aim of the latter movements

◁ An occasion which the conspirators hoped to exploit – Hitler is shown new uniforms for the Wehrmacht. On three occasions, Army volunteers in the resistance movement proposed to blow up Hitler – and themselves – by time-bombs concealed in their pockets. These men were Colonel Freiherr von Gersdorff, Captain von dem Bussche, and Captain von Kleist – son of the general. All these attempts were frustrated by Hitler's habit of suddenly changing his schedule. In this photograph the small, smiling officer at centre is General Helmuth Stieff, guardian of the conspirators' bombs – later arrested and executed.

△ Wolfsschanze–"Wolf's Lair" –Hitler's headquarters in the pine forests of Rastenburg in East Prussia. Two concentric defence perimeters screened the wooden huts and bunkers. On July 20 it was known that the Führer conference which Stauffenberg was to attend would not be held in the command bunker but in the conference hut. Although this would disperse the force of the explosion, the plotters knew that the bomb would still be powerful enough to kill Hitler.

was unequivocal: to bring an end to German occupation. Eventually this aim was expanded: to emerge from the war with far-reaching political changes in the liberated nations. There it was easy, however. The enemy was the foreigner, not the compatriot. It was a practical problem, too: the resistance leaders knew where to recruit their soldiers and their forces. Even if the actual number of men was small, the underlying cause was clear-cut and good. Everything in wartime Europe helped to justify the spirit of resistance and to trigger it into activity.

Resistance, in short, was part and parcel of the war. The underground fighters knew that the peace won by the Allies abroad would be their peace–a victorious conclusion to their own efforts in the field.

But resistance in Germany could never achieve any durable or encouraging linkup between the enemies of Hitler and the Anglo-American bloc, let alone with the Soviet bloc. This was not because no overtures were made, but because each tentative approach was rejected, for the Allied high command could not count on its orders being obeyed. Moscow formed the "Committee of Free Germany", to which belonged the generals taken at Stalingrad and the old German Communist *émigrés*. But neither London nor Washington would agree to treaties which would affect the post-war scene.

This decision of the Allies not to listen to any spokesmen from Germany discouraged many responsible Germans from taking solitary action. At the Casablanca Conference in January 1943, the Allies laid it down that the elimination of Hitler would not determine the conditions of peace. Until Casablanca, the post-war political programmes of the German opposition had all been based on the results of Germany's initial victories. Goerdeler and his friends clung to the idea that the inevitable chaos caused by Hitler's overthrow must be kept to the minimum. The basic structure of the régime would be preserved; the Party and its machine would be dismantled, but only step by step. The main ideal was not so much to reconstruct the state as to abolish the authority of the Party, together with its excesses–in other words, to cancel out the misdealt hand of 1933, when both nationalists and conservatives had been cheated. No excessive "change for the sake of change" was the watchword. In their innumerable talks Goerdeler, Beck, and their friends persuaded themselves that all they would have to do was to extend their network of loyal German malcontents, and all the loose ends would be tied up with the greatest of ease.

Dynamic leadership

At the time when Claus von Stauffenberg entered the German resistance movement, its leaders had reached an all-time low of despair and empty gestures. It was the period when the students Hans and Sophie Scholl, and their teacher, were executed at Munich for having launched an appeal for a revolt of conscience.

When Stauffenberg joined the conspirators, the idea of an attempt on Hitler's person had only just been accepted by Beck and Goerdeler. The success of such an attempt was to be followed by the entry of the Reserve Army, which would carry out the actual *coup d'état*. Of all the top-ranking commanders, Field-Marshal von Kluge seemed to be the only man willing to support the attempt. Two assassination attempts in 1943, organised by General von Tresckow, Chief-of-Staff of Army Group "Centre", had failed. And it was Tresckow who now gave Stauffenberg the relevant details.

They intended to use Plan "Valkyrie", drawn up in 1942 to mobilise the Reserve Army in the event of an insurrection by the foreign prisoners-of-war in Germany. Promoted joint Chief-of-Staff of Army Group "Centre" and stationed in Berlin, Stauffenberg spent the autumn issuing detailed orders for the *coup*. The executive order would go out from the War Ministry

continued on page 1725

▷ *The conference hut before the explosion, looking towards the end of the room from the position of the long map table.*

▽ *After the explosion. The circular table shown above has been hurled to the far end of the room. An arrow marks the spot where the bomb went off.*

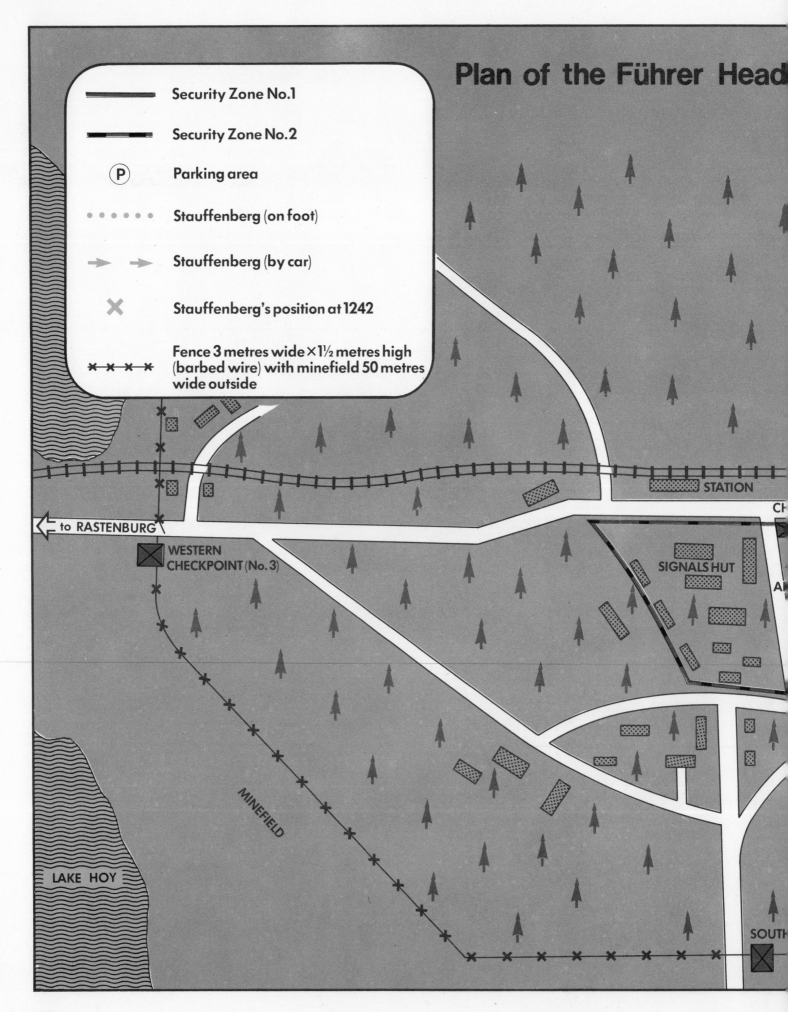

Plan of the Führer Head

Legend:

- ▬▬▬ Security Zone No.1
- ▬▬▬ Security Zone No.2
- Ⓟ Parking area
- • • • • • Stauffenberg (on foot)
- → → Stauffenberg (by car)
- ✕ Stauffenberg's position at 1242
- ✕ ✕ ✕ Fence 3 metres wide ✕1½ metres high (barbed wire) with minefield 50 metres wide outside

to RASTENBURG

WESTERN CHECKPOINT (No. 3)

SIGNALS HUT

STATION

MINEFIELD

LAKE HOY

SOUTH

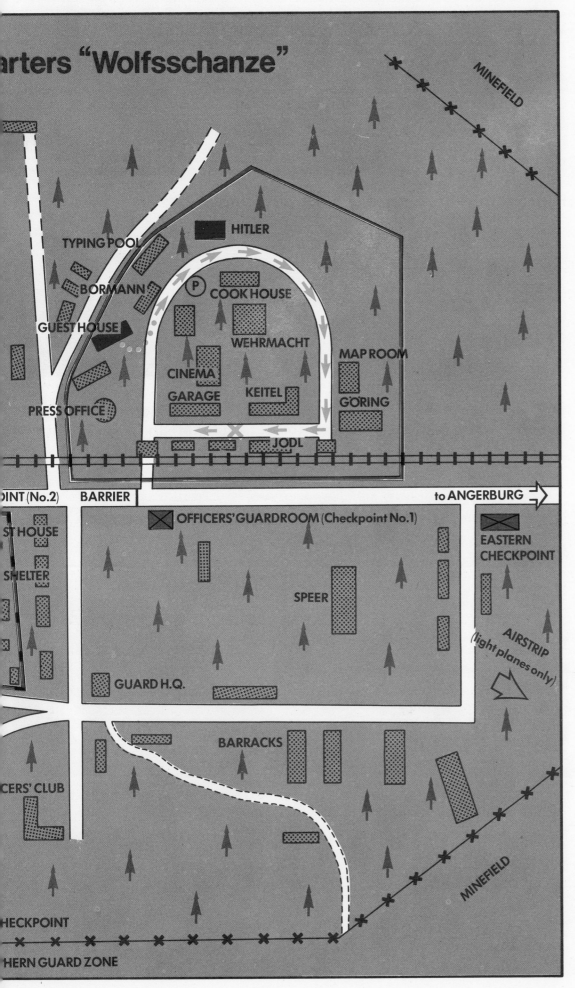

arters "Wolfsschanze"

MINEFIELD

TYPING POOL

HITLER

BORMANN

P COOK HOUSE

GUEST HOUSE

WEHRMACHT

MAP ROOM

CINEMA

GARAGE

KEITEL

GÖRING

PRESS OFFICE

JODL

POINT (No.2)   BARRIER   to ANGERBURG ➡

ST HOUSE

OFFICERS' GUARDROOM (Checkpoint No.1)

EASTERN CHECKPOINT

SHELTER

SPEER

AIRSTRIP (light planes only)

GUARD H.Q.

BARRACKS

CERS' CLUB

MINEFIELD

CHECKPOINT

HERN GUARD ZONE

How Stauffenberg and his adjutant, Lieutenant Werner von Haeften, escaped from the "Wolf's Lair" after the attempt on Hitler's life on July 20, 1944. The diagram shows the concentric security perimeters and the checkpoints through which they had to pass to make a safe getaway.

Stauffenberg's plane touched down at Rastenburg after a 3-hour flight from Berlin. A 9-mile drive lay ahead, and Stauffenberg left his pilot with instructions to be ready to take off any time after noon–the Führer conference was scheduled for 1300 hours. On arriving at the "Wolf's Lair" Stauffenberg found that the conference had been brought forward by 30 minutes, for Mussolini was arriving that afternoon and all reports at the conference were to be kept short.

While Keitel fussed at the delay, Stauffenberg returned to the ante-room to collect his cap and belt. There, using the three surviving fingers of his "good" hand, he activated the bomb.

It had a 10-minute fuse. A 3-minute walk to the conference room. Up to the big map table. Slip the briefcase under the table, as close to Hitler's feet as possible. Then a murmured excuse: a telephone call from Berlin. Out of the room, through the innermost checkpoint of "Perimeter I", and across to where Haeften was waiting.

Then, at 1242 hours by their watches, came a monstrous explosion from the hut. The two officers jumped into their car and tore round to the first checkpoint out of "Perimeter II", where Stauffenberg phoned the Duty Officer direct and obtained clearance to leave. He had no trouble at the second checkpoint, but by the time he reached the third the "Wolf's Lair" had been brought to full alert and the car was stopped. By great good luck Stauffenberg was able to persuade the Duty Officer to let him through–and the car set off at full speed for the airfield. On the way Haeften dismantled the reserve bomb and threw the pieces to the side of the road. At 1315 they were airborne for Berlin, confident not only that Hitler was dead at last but that the plotters in Berlin knew and that the *coup d'état* was in full swing.

But it was not.

1723

Mussolini: "What has happened here today gives me new courage. After this miracle it is inconceivable that our cause should meet with misfortune."

Hitler: "It is obvious that nothing is going to happen to me; undoubtedly it is my fate to continue on my way and bring my task to completion."

continued from page 1720

once the definite news of Hitler's death had been received. The key centres of the capital would be occupied and the S.S. put under Army control, voluntarily or by force. The chain of command would be reorganised.

Precise, far-sighted, and quick-thinking, Stauffenberg introduced into the conspiracy a dynamism which no officer before him had shown. Level-headed, impatient of political theories, and flexible in his approach both to men and events, he gradually became the rallying-point for the resistance elements which had hitherto remained at loggerheads. Weighing the problems, always trying to find a balance, he insisted on "possible compromises and points of joint agreement, without contradictions". But Stauffenberg's flexibility of spirit and his optimism could and did lead him astray. He was hardly being realistic, for example, when on May 25, 1944 he drew up a list of topics to be discussed with the Allied high command. These included the following:

1. The Eastern Front to be held; all occupied areas in the North, West, and South to be evacuated;
2. The Allies to abandon all projects for the occupation of Germany; and
3. Eastern European frontiers to be restored to the *status quo* of 1914, Austria and the Sudetenland to remain part of the Reich, but autonomy for Alsace-Lorraine.

The conspirators clung to the hope of an alliance between the Western Allies and the Reich against the Soviet Union. "To save what remains of our military power to allow Germany to continue to play a part in the international power balance"—such was Stauffenberg's intention until the Allies landed on D-Day.

Since autumn 1943 several more assassination attempts had failed. The plans had been reworked and the conspirators extended their contacts throughout the Reich and the occupied territories. At the end of May 1944, Stauffenberg was appointed chief-of-staff at the high command of the Reserve Army in Berlin—a post which kept him in the capital, but which nevertheless permitted him to take part in certain discussions at Hitler's headquarters.

The Allied landings in Normandy on June 6, 1944, wrecked Stauffenberg's hopes that his country would be left at least some freedom of manoeuvre. The assassination attempt must take place,

◁ and ◁▽ Hitler greets Mussolini at Rastenburg—the Duce arrived within hours of the explosion—and shows him the scene of the "miracle". This was the last time the two dictators met.

▽ Göring visits the shattered hut and congratulates Hitler on his "providential" escape.

Tresckow urged. Every day that passed would make it more complicated. There was no more time in which to look for the right man. Stauffenberg decided to act himself.

July 20

July 11. July 13. Two more postponements. And then, on July 20, Stauffenberg at last managed to leave his briefcase, containing a time-bomb, within feet of Hitler in the conference-room at O.K.H. headquarters in East Prussia. After hearing the explosion from outside, he flew back to Berlin. The order went out. "Valkyrie" was in force. Or so Stauffenberg believed.

At 1600 hours Beck finally arrived at the War Ministry at the *Bendlerstrasse* in Berlin. It was still not certain that Hitler was dead – but no matter. Prompt action was needed to take over Berlin.

The last hours of the 20th passed in total confusion, of which Hitler and his supporters took full advantage. The commander of the battalion on guard duty, uncertain as to which orders he should obey, was put directly in touch with Hitler by Goebbels. He was told to restore order.

As night fell the conspirators saw their hesitant allies abandon them, one by one. Stauffenberg, unshaken, ordered all the plans to be carried out. But at 2300 hours Fromm, C.-in-C. of the Reserve Army, surrounded by officers of the guard, arrested the last conspirators: Colonel Mertz von Quirnheim, General Olbricht, Stauffenberg, and Lieutenant Haeften.

They were hurried outside and shot.

But this was only the beginning. Hitler's revenge was immediate. Some 200 suspects, closely or remotely implicated in the plot, were hideously executed – hanged from meathooks on piano-wire nooses, their death agonies being filmed for Hitler – mostly at Plötzensee Prison in Berlin.

A few days before July 20, Stauffenberg had declared to one of his friends: "The time has come to do something. But whoever has the courage to do it must realise that he will probably be branded as a traitor in future German histories. Yet if he declines to act he will only be a traitor in his own conscience."

When all is said and done, every verdict on the political and military intentions of the conspirators, and on their chances of success, must give place to this comment, which Stauffenberg justified by his death.

△ Huddled in a cloak, Hitler takes a constitutional at Rastenburg with Himmler at his side. The Reichsführer-S.S. was given the task of hunting down the conspirators and bringing them to book.

Was the attempt on Hitler's life on July 20, 1944, based on any genuine national desire to rid the German nation of the man who was leading it to ruin? Or was it, as the Nazi propagandists maintained, merely the work of foresworn malcontents and traitors to whom their solemn oath of allegiance meant nothing?

The first point to note is that the civil and military personnel who took part in the plot operated largely in isolation not only from the mass of the German people, but also from their fellow-officers in the Army. The plot had its roots in the German aristocracy, especially in the Prussian nobility, in the upper middle classes, and in certain intellectual, university, and religious circles which had little to do with the ordinary people, and the savage repression of the uprising aroused

no feeling of reprobation or even of sympathy in the majority of the nation.

Was this silent disavowal of the conspirators by a majority of the German people the result of Goebbels's propaganda and the terror caused by Himmler's police? It must have been. But Anglo-Saxon propaganda also played its part by implying as it did that workers and peasants would unite in punishing Hitler and his accomplices, whereas the systematic destruction of the cities of the Third Reich, causing thousands of civilian casualties every day, only strengthened the régime's grip on the people, both morally and materially.

The officers concerned in the plot came solely from the Army. Göring controlled all promotions in the Luftwaffe and therefore had all his officers

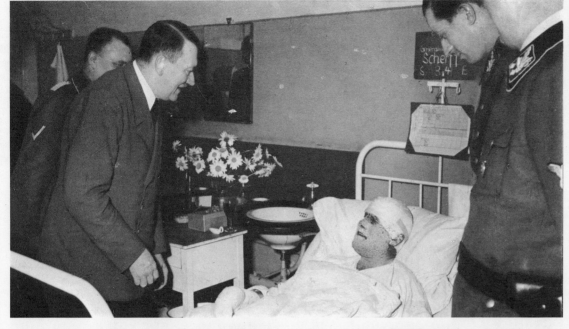

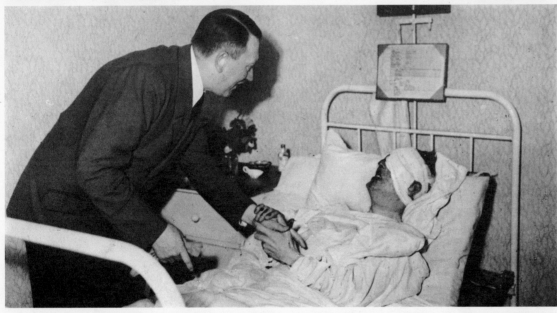

on a tight rein. The Navy, like most navies throughout the world, was apolitical, and its personnel, whether at sea or in harbour in Norway, France, or Italy, had no idea of the atrocities perpetrated by the régime and only a vague suspicion of the catastrophe about to break on the Eastern Front.

The conspirators

No general with a command on the Eastern Front seems to have been implicated. Field-Marshals Rommel and von Kluge, General Carl Heinrich von Stülpnagel, the military commander in France, and Lieutenant-General Speidel, chief-of-staff of Army Group "B", had all taken part

at least in the plot aimed at the overthrow of the régime if not in the attempt on Hitler's life engineered by Lieutenant-Colonel Claus Schenk von Stauffenberg. In Paris, at a given signal, Stülpnagel was to neutralise the Gestapo; at la Roche-Guyon, Rommel was to get in touch with Montgomery with a view to an armistice on the Western Front.

At O.K.H. the two front-rank men were Generals Wagner and Fellgiebel. The former was Quartermaster-General and the latter head of communications and, as such, had the job, once the explosion was heard, of putting out of action the Rastenburg telephone exchange and radio station. In Berlin Field-Marshal von Witzleben, Rundstedt's predecessor at Saint Germain-en-Laye, Colonel-General Ludwig Beck, former Army Chief-of-

△△ ◁ *Hitler at the bedside of General Scherff.*
△ ◁ *The dying General Schmundt, Hitler's adjutant since the outbreak of war, clasps the Führer's hand. A plug of cotton wool at Hitler's ear bears witness to his perforated eardrum.*
△△ *and* △ *Shredded uniforms of bomb plot victims, displayed with grim relish for the Nazi records.*

BEFORE THE PEOPLE'S COURT

ACCUSED: I thought of the many murders—

FREISLER: Murders?

ACCUSED: At home and abroad—

FREISLER: You really are a low scoundrel. Are you breaking down under this rottenness? Yes or no—are you breaking down under it?

ACCUSED: Herr President!

FREISLER: Yes or no, a clear answer!

ACCUSED: No.

FREISLER: Nor can you break down any more. For you are nothing but a small heap of misery that has no respect for itself any longer.

◁ ◁ and ◁ Two of the civilian conspirators in court: Delp (left) and Goerdeler.
◁ ◁ ◁ Freisler, President of the People's Court, promised Hitler "draconian justice". The Führer called him "our Vishinsky".
◁ ◁▽ A session of the court. Under glaring lights (the hearings were filmed) the accused stood alone against the torrent of abuse pouring from Freisler. Technicians grumbled that Freisler's yelling made a decent recording job almost impossible.

◁ Witzleben takes the stand, struggling with the baggy suit (minus belt) which he had been given to make him look ridiculous. "You disgusting old man!" bellowed Freisler. "Stop fiddling about with your trousers!"

◁ Hoeppner, disgraced by Hitler after the battle of Moscow and forbidden to wear uniform. Like Witzleben, he was hanged.

△ and ▷▷ Rommel, Germany's most famous general, had supported the plotters and was fatally implicated when they failed. The man who had once commanded Hitler's bodyguard, seen above as Hitler congratulated him for the capture of Tobruk, must die— but it was hoped that the embarrassment of a People's Court trial could be avoided. Rommel, still convalescing at home from his wounds suffered in Normandy, was visited by two O.K.H. officers. They gave him the choice between a cyanide capsule, a "heart attack", a state funeral, and generous care for his wife and son—or the humiliation of public disgrace. He chose the former, told his wife and son that he would be dead in 15 minutes, and drove off with the officers. The whole ghastly charade was carried out as promised, with wreaths from Hitler, Goebbels, and Göring; and Rundstedt pronouncing the funeral oration. ▷▷▽ Rommel's death mask, preserving the look of contempt on his face as he died.

Staff who resigned over the Sudeten crisis, Colonel-General Hoeppner, relieved of his command of the 4th *Panzerarmee* in January 1942 for completely specious reasons, Colonel-General Fromm, commanding the *Ersatzheer* (units in the process of formation within the Reich), and General von Hase, the military commander of the capital, were all to exploit immediately the success of the attempt.

We know that Hitler escaped by a miracle when the time-bomb, left in a brief-case by Stauffenberg, went off at his feet. Goebbels's determination and Major Remer's discipline, together with a battalion of infantry, were then enough to put an end to the Berlin conspirators. This shows how little this plot, hatched by a handful of generals and general staff officers, scarcely known to the soldiery and even less to the country, had taken root in the Army.

Criticism from all sides

Not only the fanatics of the régime and Hitler's toadies, but also Manstein, Dönitz, and Guderian openly criticised the plot. They did so for moral and patriotic reasons, the value of which might be questioned given the situation of the moment, but which must be admitted as well-founded in principle.

Apropos of the attempt to overthrow the government by force, Field-Marshal von Manstein, even though unjustly disgraced by Hitler, was not afraid to say:

"I will merely say that I did not think that, in my position as a responsible military leader, I had to envisage the idea of a *coup d'état* which, in my opinion, would have led to a rapid collapse of the front and brought Germany to chaos. Not to mention, of course, the question of the oath or the legitimacy and the right of committing murder for political reasons. As I stated at my trial: 'One cannot, as a military leader, for years call upon soldiers to sacrifice their lives for victory and then bring about defeat by one's own actions.' On the other hand it was already clear that a *coup d'état* would not have changed in any way the Allies' determination to demand unconditional surrender from Germany."

Grand-Admiral Dönitz, though he did not refuse to recognise that the July 20 conspirators had a "moral justification" for what they did, "particularly if they were privy to the mass murders ordered by the Hitler régime", nevertheless criticised their actions for the following reason:

"The mass of the people was behind Hitler. It did not know the facts which had determined the plotters to act. The elimination of Hitler in itself was not enough to destroy the National Socialist state. Its organisms could be expected to rise against any new government. There would be internal chaos. The front would be severely weakened. It would receive no more reinforcements or supplies. Under these conditions the soldiers could only repudiate any overthrow of authority. Their officers were constantly being called upon to ask them to sacrifice their lives. Could they then support an act which, by weakening the front, would make conditions more difficult for their hard-pressed men?"

He added: "There is no doubt that the authors of the attempt were grievously wrong in their concept of what was to be expected from abroad. It would not have altered in any way the enemy's determination to obtain 'unconditional surrender'. Hitler's death would not have stopped the flow of blood as many thought."

This is also in line with Colonel-General Guderian's thinking. "Evidently," he wrote, "the question is still being

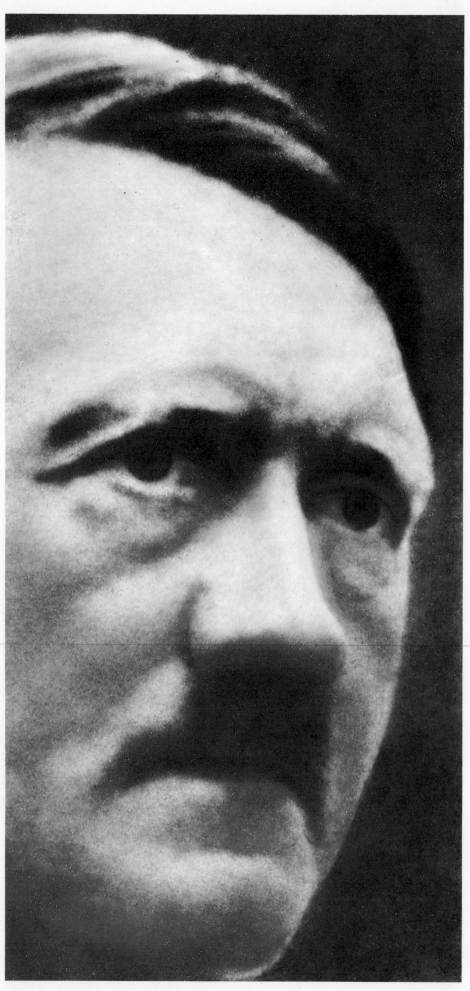

"It is a gang of criminal elem we shall settle accounts with are accustomed."

asked: 'What would have happened if the attempt had succeeded?' No one can say. One thing seems certain, however: at the time a great majority of the German people still believed in Adolf Hitler; they would have been convinced that the authors of the plot had removed the only man perhaps capable of bringing the war to an honourable conclusion. The whole odium would have fallen on the officer corps in the first place, on the generals and the general staff, both during the war and after. The hatred and the scorn of the people would have been turned against the soldiers who, in the midst of a life and death struggle, would have been thought to have broken their oath to the flag and to have removed the pilot of the ship of state in peril by assassinating the supreme leader of the Reich. For this reason it is improbable that our enemies would have treated us any better than they did after we were defeated."

These criticisms of the July conspirators, men of honour and integrity, take us back to the arguments about the legitimacy of tyrannicide so common in the Middle Ages and during the Renaissance.

"Providence has protected me so well from all harm that I can continue to labour on the great task of victory." It was in these terms that Hitler announced to the German people that he had emerged practically unharmed from the attempt on his life which killed General Schmundt, his A.D.C., General Korten, Chief-of-Staff of the Luftwaffe, and several other people in his entourage.

But what paths would the aforesaid Providence take to bring the Third Reich to final victory through the instrument of its miraculously-saved leader? During the first half of this year it had been the *matériel* and moral action of his missiles which Hitler had used to give heart to his generals. The liberation of Normandy, then Picardy, the Pas-de-Calais and Flanders, had then put London out of range of the V-1 flying bombs, so now he called upon the ghost of Frederick the Great when he summoned his generals around him or received one of them in his office.

At the end of 1761 everyone thought that Frederick's cause was hopelessly lost, in spite of the King's military genius, as six years of the vicissitudes of war and the eventual enormous superiority of the coalition of Austria, France, and Russia had brought the little Prussian kingdom to its knees. By December 26 it all seemed over when Providence disposed of the Tsarina Elizabeth and brought to the throne of Russia the Prussophile Peter III, who came to terms with Frederick behind the backs of his allies on May 5 and June 19, 1762. Discouraged by this defection, Louis XV and Maria Theresa threw their hand in and on February 15, 1763 recognised Frederick's occupation of Silesia.

Frederick, by holding on in spite of all appearances to the contrary had, by his genius, prevailed over those of his counsellors who had advised him to give in and thus reaped the reward of his perseverance. Exactly the same point had been reached in 1944. The unnatural coalition between the Soviet Union and the Anglo-Saxons could dissolve at any

moment. The Red Army's enormous daily successes could only accelerate the process as Stalin would be unable to resist the temptation of Constantinople and the Straits, which would inevitably arouse the hostility of Great Britain.

Improbable as it may seem, this was the way Hitler's thoughts ran during the night of September 12-13 in conversations with Colonel-General Friessner, who was striving to keep the Russians out of the Hungarian plain after the "defection" of Rumania and Bulgaria. To his utter amazement, Friessner was told by Hitler that *"Germany was no longer the political objective of the Soviets, but the Bosporus. That was how things stood now.* The U.S.S.R. was going to put the Balkans and the Bosporus first. Within a fortnight, or at the latest within six weeks, there would be a major clash of Allied interests in these areas. Germany must therefore expect the war *to take a decisive turn to her advantage.* England had clearly no interest in seeing Germany razed to the ground; on the contrary she needed *Germany as a buffer state.* But Germany

◁ *Still absolute warlord, even if he did need a magnifying glass to see where to draw the arrows on the map of his shrinking empire.*

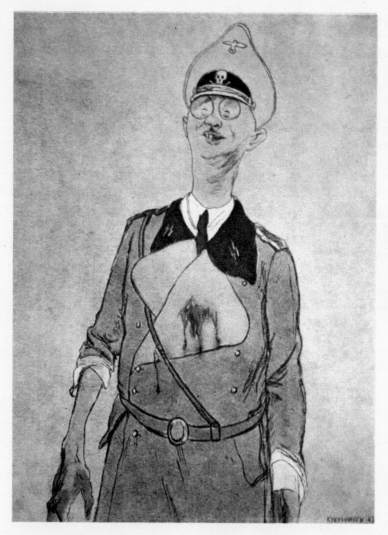

△ *Savage Russian caricatures of the two Nazi leaders who did most to crush the July Plot and defame its adherents: Himmler and Goebbels.*

had to gain time: every effort should be made to hold the Balkan fronts."

Hitler's conclusions were evidently based on two hypotheses at which he had arrived arbitrarily, as was his custom:
1. that Stalin would march on Constantinople without more ado, and
2. that Britain which, in his opinion, was the dominant partner in the Anglo-Saxon alliance, would try to stop him by force.

But Stalin was to wait for the liquidation of Germany before turning to the Turkish narrows. And everybody knew that between Roosevelt and Churchill the British Prime Minister did not have the last word.

Hitler's vengeance

At this juncture, however, no one dared to contradict Hitler. The failure of the July 20 plot allowed him to wreak terrible vengeance on the German Army. Seventeen generals were executed, the luckiest of them shot, the others hanged with atrocious refinements of cruelty and publicity. Field-Marshals von Kluge and Rommel, Colonel-General Beck, General Wagner, Major-General von Tresckow, chief-of-staff of the 2nd Army, took poison or shot themselves.

A wave of terror swept through the Army. To keep a tighter rein on his generals, Hitler took their families as hostages, returning to the principle of collective responsibility, a throwback to the ancient German custom. *Reichsführer* Heinrich Himmler was appointed head of the *Ersatzheer* in place of Colonel-General Fromm, whilst the faithful Dr. Goebbels was given the job of organising total mobilisation. The military salute was replaced by the Hitler salute and the party appointed political commissars in units and headquarters, to be responsible for the supervision and National Socialist indoctrination of the fighting troops.

And so the Führer controlled all the means of pressure which would allow him to change a military defeat, 1918 style, into a national catastrophe in which not a single inch of the soil of the Fatherland would be spared.

THE PROPAGANDA WAR

GOEBBELS: The arch-priest

The name of Joseph Goebbels will always be firmly linked with the theory and practice of propaganda. His brilliant use of the German language to "sell" National Socialism to the German people cannot be denied. A fanatically faithful Nazi, he remained loyal to Hitler until the end; his task, of implanting that loyalty in every citizen of the Third Reich, was faithfully and effectively carried out.

Goebbels was in one sense a rarity in the Nazi Party; he had a university education behind him. In point of fact he had attended eight universities –all of them in the first rank of German learning–by the time he had graduated from Heidelberg in 1921 with a Ph.D., at the age of 24. He was a devoted and impassioned nationalist, with superimposed bitterness due to his crippled left leg, the result of osteomyelitis at the age of seven followed by an unsuccessful operation. In 1922, having heard Hitler speak at Munich, Goebbels joined the Nazi Party.

Despite a succession of rabble-rousing speeches against the French occupation of the Ruhr (he was a Rhinelander himself, born at Rheydt in 1897), it took some three years for Goebbels to make his mark in the Party. And when he did it was as a protégé of Gregor Strasser, leading Nazi radical who put far too much emphasis on the socialist part of National Socialism for Hitler's liking. Matters came to a head when the Strasser-Goebbels faction of the Party pressed for a link-up with the Communists in a programme to deprive the surviving royalty and nobility of their hereditary possessions.

Hitler, however, won back Goebbels at Munich in April 1926. He turned the full blast of his personality on Goebbels, inspiring the latter to flights of near-hysterical hero-worship from which he never departed again.

Master-speaker though he was, with a fine voice and razor-keen sense of timing, Goebbels was no mere tub-thumper for the Party. He played a key rôle in unsavoury but crucial operations such as the firing of the Reichstag and the anti-Röhm "Blood Purge", not to mention taking decisive action to contain and round up the Army plotters in Berlin after the failure of the 1944 "July Plot".

He kept faith until the end, killing his family and committing suicide with his wife in the Berlin *Führerbunker* in 1945.

◁ ◁ *At the microphone: the master in action.*
◁ *The Minister at his desk.*
▽ ◁ *Public relations work, standard for Nazi leaders: beaming over a small child.*
▽ *Party official on parade, radiating devotion to the Führer.*

This page: *The distinctive Kukryniksy style compared with similar efforts abroad.*
◁ *Stockholm's* Sondagnisse Strix *shows Himmler and Goebbels keeping a tight hold on "General Scapegoat"–keeping him in reserve for when the Führer's intuition results in a defeat.*
▽ ◁ *Kukryniksy par excellence. Goebbels shrilly claims more smashing victories in Russia. And a wooden echo from the row of coffined Wehrmacht troops adds: "We hope for more successes in the future . . ."*
▽ *Bance Russell of the* New York Post *adopts the simian look for his version of Goebbels.*

▷ *Before the Non-Aggression Pact: capitalism, fond godfathers of Nazism–France, Britain, Wall Street, and the industrial magnates of the Ruhr.*
▽ ▷ *Munich time, 1938: the dictators and the appeasers.*

1740

RUSSIA: savage and hard-hitting

When Germany invaded the Soviet Union in June 1941, Russian propagandists had to make a swift about-turn. Ever since the Non-Aggression Pact of 1939 they had been following the Molotov line: war with Germany was contrary to the mutual interests of the two countries. Operation "Barbarossa" put an abrupt end to that.

The savagery with which the Russian propagandists fell upon the invading "Hitlerite hordes" was a faithful by-product of the Russo-German war; but in many ways the Russian technique had been foreshadowed. One of the most obvious examples was the caricaturists' treatment of the Nazi leaders – Hitler the villain of the piece, the wolf in sheep's clothing with dripping fangs; Himmler with his headsman's axe; Goebbels wizened, monkey-like (with or without tail, according to choice). There are two fair examples of this general similarity on the opposite page, one from Stockholm and one from America.

One of the key principles of modern propaganda was summed up by Lewis Carroll's Humpty Dumpty in *Alice:* "When *I* use a word it means exactly what I intend it to mean; neither more nor less." And nowhere was this more true than in the original Soviet propaganda before the Ribbentrop pact of 1939. Russian propaganda in the 1930s screamed of the growing menace of Nazidom and the cowardice of the Western democracies in failing to tackle the Axis dictators head-on.

In the first months of the German invasion there was all too little for Russian propagandists to cheer about. Bedrock appeals to Russian nationalism – "The Motherland Calls!" – were ranged beside hard-hitting criticism of Nazi brutality. An early theme to emerge from the Kukryniksy team of caricaturists was "the training of Fritz" – a Nazi boyhood, from torturing cats as a young boy, beating up old folk in the Hitler Youth, and finally emerging with his blood-spattered ceremonial axe, all ready for service in Russia.

Then came Moscow in December 1941, and a clear-cut victory. At once a theme emerged which would remain a constant stand-by: the theme of Russian might, represented by a gigantic pair of pincers carving deep into the emaciated German lines, or a massive, monolithic tank.

After Stalingrad came another new style. This was the personification of the Red Army soldier: a young giant with a stern and vengeful expression, sweeping the Germans before him with a broom made of bayonets. It was a fair reflection of the deliberate glorification of the Red Army in the post-Stalingrad era, when the long chain of victories began.

Stalin's propagandists were also quick to exploit the many sieges of Russian capitals and provincial centres – Odessa, Leningrad, Moscow, Stalingrad, Sevastopol'. As with the British victims of the Blitz, this identified the urban population with the front-line troops, with battle honours of their own of which they could be proud.

△ *Kukryniksy jeer at Hitler after Moscow, or, the* Blitzkrieg *drum bursts.*

◁ *Past enemies of "Mother Russia" preserved as a warning. From left to right: one of the Teutonic Knights repelled by Alexander Nevsky; Charles XII of Sweden, defeated by Peter the Great; Napoleon; Hitler; and a Japanese Samurai, the last being a reference to the brisk frontier war with Japan fought in 1938-39.*

▷ *Decline of the Axis, 1941-44.*

The German recovery after Stalingrad inspired a natural note of caution among the Russian propagandists; but then came Kursk, the turning-point on the Eastern Front, and the era of the massed "victory salutes" in Moscow began. But the image of the "Nazi beast" remained, and there were two obvious reasons for this. The first was the discovery of German atrocities in the territories liberated by the Red Army; the second was the tenacity of the Wehrmacht in defence, which grew ever more ferocious as it fell back on the frontiers of the Reich.

These two factors inspired the notorious "hate propaganda" of Ilya Ehrenburg. "We cannot live as long as these grey-green slugs are alive. Today there are no books; today there are no stars in the sky; today there is only one thought: Kill the Germans. Kill them all and dig them into the earth." And again: "We are remembering everything. Now we know. The Germans are not human. Now the word 'German' has become the most terrible swear-word. Let us not speak. Let us not be indignant. Let us kill . . . If you have killed one German, kill another. There is nothing jollier than German corpses."

Ehrenburg's "hate propaganda" was maintained at red-hot intensity right through to the spring of 1945. As the invasion of the Reich proceeded he was writing: "The Fritzes are still running, but not lying dead. Who can stop us now? General Model? The Oder? The Volkssturm? No, it's too late. Germany, you can now whirl round in circles, and burn, and howl in your deathly agony; the hour of revenge has struck!" But by April 1945 it was increasingly obvious that "hate propaganda" was out of date in view of Germany's imminent collapse and the post-war problems of administering the occupied sectors of the Reich; and Ehrenburg was abruptly muzzled. His "hate propaganda" had served its turn; now it was not only outdated but a positive embarrassment.

As the string of Russian victories lengthened, ridicule began to emerge more and more in Russian posters and cartoons. The Nazi beast tended to give place to the tattered scarecrow, emaciated, ridiculous, but never quite pathetic.

Being as it was the product of a totalitarian state, Russian propaganda was manipulated with stone-faced cynicism and little scope was given to individual viewpoints. The "official line" remained all-important. Yet Russian propaganda never lost its edge. Right to the end it remained ruthless and hard-hitting, with a style all its own. From the months of defeat to final victory, these characteristics remained.

△ △ "The Nazi beast aboard his tank"–standard Kukryniksy view of the German invaders down to Stalingrad.

△ "The tired old organ-grinder takes to the road"–ridicule takes over. Hitler shambles from the scene with Mussolini and Rumania's Antonescu as his performing monkeys.

▷ Moscow, 1941–and the first genuine note of confidence. Russia's field army is portrayed as an invincible pair of pincers. The same motif would be repeated many times when other sieges were raised–most notably in the case of Leningrad, with vengeful swords slicing through the shrinking German arms encircling the city.

▷ ▷ "The Führer is beside himself"–derisive Kukryniksy jibe at the shaky relations between the Führer and his commanding generals. The surrenders at Stalingrad gave the Russians plenty of opportunities to weigh up these weaknesses for themselves.

BRITAIN: the straight-faced look

British propaganda stands out in total contrast with the Russian style. For this there are many reasons. The first is the basic uncertainty with which Britain went to war, an uncertainty compounded by the months of "Phoney War". Clearly Nazism was to be destroyed, and this programme was always confidently featured. Much more important, however, was the fact that Britain was quite unready for war; hence the dominant stream of poster campaigns aimed at getting the country onto a war footing by urging economies of every sort in the home.

The Blitz gave British propaganda its first genuine boost. Now the war was being brought home to the British people in a new and hateful way: anonymously and impartially, by the bomber. The British may not have had the Nazi invader on their soil, enslaving and torturing; but they did have "Firebomb Fritz" and the murderers of Coventry. The same applied to the German U-boat offensive in the Atlantic, which triggered off many a "Careless Talk" campaign as well as representing the German submariners as cowardly assassins.

Nevertheless the British war effort remained essentially insular. Even the intense campaigns aimed at whipping up support for Russia after the German invasion in 1941 were aimed largely at exploiting socialist and working-class enthusiasm in the factory. "Tanks for Russia" was typical.

In the leaflet war against German civilians and servicemen the British approach remained generally naïve. The trouble here was that until the end of 1942 the Germans were obviously winning the war, and even in 1943 it was far from obvious that they were going to lose it. Sir David Hunt, with the 8th Army, has commented on the difficulties that propagandists encountered in the field. "They were hampered a little by the fact that their only means of delivering pamphlets was to replace with them the smoke cartridge of a 25-pounder, base-ejection smoke shell. This meant that the inspiring and carefully-chosen words had to be squashed on to a round piece of paper just a little over three inches in diameter and with a circular hole in the middle. So far as I remember the most that space allowed was something like this: 'Dear Germans—why not stop fighting? We will really treat you quite well.'"

Not surprisingly, they failed.

▽ Drab reality: the typical appearance of British war-time propaganda, hardly redolent of a crusade for the rights and freedom of mankind.
▷ Before the "Phoney War" removed the gloves: bold type and bald message.

1746

1747

Beat
'FIREBOMB
FRITZ'
BRITAIN
SHALL NOT
BURN
BRITAIN'S FIRE GUARD IS BRITAIN'S DEFENCE

CASTLES OF THE AIR

Man the walls!

Join a BALLOON BARRAGE SQUADRON

AUXILIARY AIR FORCE

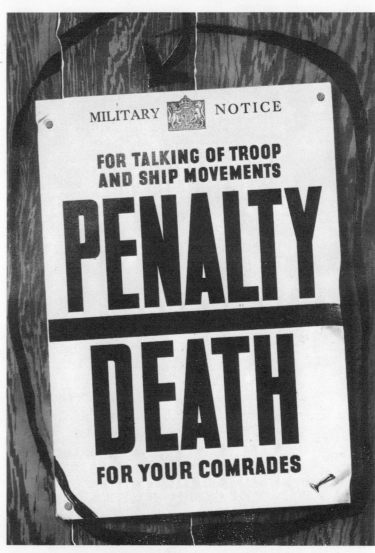

MILITARY NOTICE

FOR TALKING OF TROOP AND SHIP MOVEMENTS

PENALTY

DEATH

FOR YOUR COMRADES

It all depends on YOU - GO TO IT!

THE GLORIOUS END OF THE "GLOWWORM." This destroyer, one YOU helped to build, engaged a force of enemy cruisers and destroyers in Norwegian waters and went down fighting.

SHIPS, TANKS and LORRIES are the FORCES' URGENT NEED
CARRY ON AT TOP SPEED!

THORNYCROFT

◁ ◁ *When the war came home to the British: the bogey of the Blitz.*

△ ◁ *Attractive and comforting, but hardly aggressive: an appeal for balloon barrage volunteers.*

△ *"Careless talk" posters were ubiquitous. This is a particularly strong variant.*

◁ *Supply minister Herbert Morrison coined one of the best home front slogans of the war: "Go to it!" This exhortation was extended to almost every facet of the British war effort.*

Entente cordiale!

However, as the war progressed the British developed considerable skill in the field of "black" propaganda. As opposed to "white" propaganda–the traditional medium–"black" propaganda had a subtlety which often bordered on the fiendish. One form was the "*Kreisleiter* letter". German parents would receive a fake document regretfully informing them that their son had been killed in action on such and such a day, and that his personal effects had been forwarded home to his local *Kreisleiter*. Naturally the *Kreisleiter,* when approached, would know nothing about the dead soldier's possessions. It was an ingenious way of using enemy battle casualties to undermine faith in the Nazi régime.

Then there was *Soldatensender Calais,* a broadcasting station aimed at the German troops in Western Europe. This was put to good use before and after D-Day, undermining German morale with grim warnings of what was coming and depressing news of what the continuation of the war was doing to their homes. *Soldatensender Calais* used tough

The Mediterranean Invasion. British troops, tanks guns pouring ashore from landing craft.

VICTORY OF THE ALLIES IS ASSURED

THE RED ARMY'S Fight is YOUR Fight!

The Communist Party says **ACT NOW!**

★ *Remove Pro-fascists from high places*
★ *End Employers' Mismanagement and Waste*
★ *Restore T.U. Rights and "Daily Worker"*

AID SOVIET—SMASH HITLER!

soldier's jargon and pulled no punches. It was obviously a foreign station—that was the point.

It must be concluded that the "black" approaches proved to be the most skilful refinement of British propaganda. In the more conventional media, the British technique always seems to have been too polite.

△ *Axis subtlety: the "Big Three" alliance corroded by the American dollar, for the benefit of the occupied French.*
△▷ *British sobriety: once again, the direct approach.*
▷ *A blast from the British Communist Party—with the Red Army coming off second best to trades union rights and the Daily Worker.*

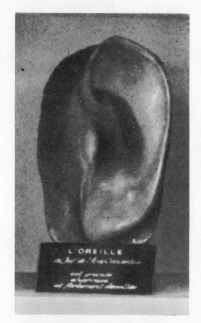

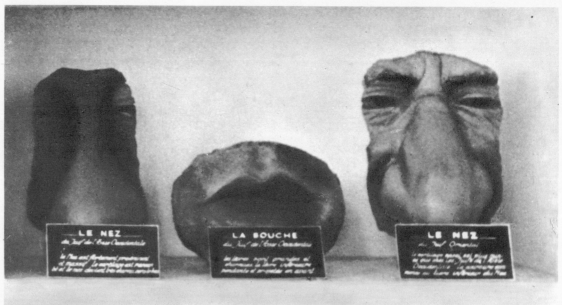

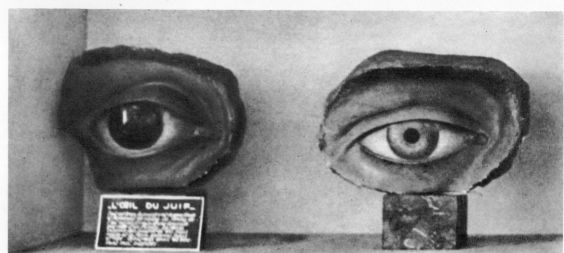

△ and ▷ "Every Frenchman who is determined to combat the Hebrew menace must learn how to recognise the Jew." These so-called "Jewish features" were put on public display as part of the anti-Semitic programme in France. ▷▷ Poster for a public exhibition: "The Jew and France."

THE JEWS: prime victims

Anti-Semitism had always been a classic Nazi plank, and it necessarily motivated a great deal of propaganda. From the earliest day of the German Nazi Party's career Jew-hating was urged on all "good Germans" by the Party's propagandists. The most notorious was the bullying Julius Streicher, "Jew-baiter No. 1", and his illustrated paper *Der Stürmer*. This nauseating publication was tireless in churning out the worst in anti-Semitism, vacillating between the incredibly childish and the brutally obscene.

But the crudity of *Der Stürmer* was only a very small part of the anti-Jewish programme. Behind the street-corner roaring and bullying lay the horror of the pseudo-scientific attempts to prove for ever that "Aryans" were the master-race and Jews the source of all corruption and degeneracy. What Churchill referred to as "the lights of perverted science" applied precisely to this aspect of the anti-Jewish programme; and the display casts of so-called "typically Jewish features" shown above are an excellent example.

Playing on anti-Semitic instincts was an inevitable part of the Nazi policy towards occupied countries. In France, for example, a mass of anti-Jewish material appeared, fit to gladden the heart of Streicher himself.

It is a curious fact that very little propaganda appeared as a counter-blast to the Nazi anti-Semitic programme. After all, there is little that can be said to refute the vicious generalisations which were the Nazis' stock-in-trade than to quote and condemn them. It has to be admitted that "Save the Jews" never emerged as a dominant Allied propaganda line. Appeals to patriotism; exhortations to enlist, to work harder; condemnations of certified enemy atrocities –these carried more weight and predominated in public propaganda during World War II. It should also be remembered that the tangible evidence of the full extent of the "Final Solution" –the death camps–was not brought to the public eye until the closing months of the war. So it was that one of the grimmest aspects of the war remained largely an Axis prerogative in the powerful sphere of propaganda.

MICHEL JACQUOT
SEPTEMBRE - OCTOBRE
EXPOSITION
LE JUIF
ET LA FRANCE
PALAIS BERLITZ . 31 Bd DES ITALIENS

ORLD CONQUEST

"A LOWER RACE NEEDS LESS ROOM, LESS CLOTHING, LESS FOOD, AND LESS CULTURE THAN A HIGHER RACE. THE GERMAN CANNOT LIVE UNDER THE SAME CONDITIONS AS THE POLE OR THE JEW." DR. ROBERT LEY, THE LEADER OF THE GERMAN LABOR FRONT IN THE ANGRIFF ON JANUARY 31, 1940.

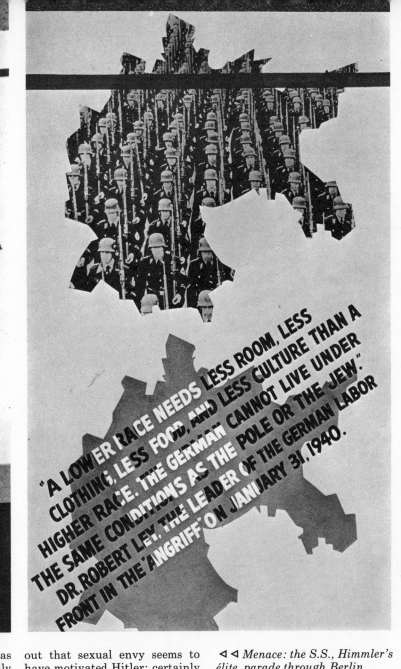

"A LOWER RACE NEEDS LESS ROOM, LESS CLOTHING, LESS FOOD, AND LESS CULTURE THAN A HIGHER RACE. THE GERMAN CANNOT LIVE UNDER THE SAME CONDITIONS AS THE POLE OR THE JEW." DR. ROBERT LEY, THE LEADER OF THE GERMAN LABOR FRONT IN THE ANGRIFF ON JANUARY 31, 1940.

Mein Kampf was the Nazi bible and enshrined Hitler's anti-Semitic fetish. He wallowed in it. When he told of his fastidious reactions to pre-1914 Vienna he really plumbed the depths. "Was there any form of filth or profligacy, particularly in cultural life," he shrieked in *Mein Kampf*, "without at least one Jew involved in it? If you cut even cautiously into such an abscess, you found, like a maggot in a rotting body, often dazzled by the sudden light – a yid!"

"Gradually," Hitler solemnly went on, "I began to hate them." The tragedy was that he was not alone, that the hate-ridden tripe of *Mein Kampf* was retailed to the German public with consummate ease. The sales of *Mein Kampf* made Hitler a millionaire. The book was second only to the Bible in the number of copies sold in Nazi Germany. The book was ostentatiously displayed in the homes of the prudent and was solemnly presented to the happy couple at weddings.

What made matters worse was that *Mein Kampf* is such a badly written book that few people – let alone Germans – managed to read it thoroughly. For it conceals nothing of Hitler's long-term plans for Germany and the German-dominated world to which he aspired. It was the blueprint for the "Final Solution", the total eradication of Jewry which was the only logical goal of the Nazi creed. *Mein Kampf* was published for the first time in the autumn of 1925 – but as early as that Hitler was laying down that argument that the spaces of eastern Europe – and Russia – were the only areas into which Germany could and must expand.

One of the most unpleasant aspects of the Nazi brand of Jew-baiting was its obsession with sexual corruption. Here again Hitler took the lead in *Mein Kampf*, accusing the Jews of being at the heart of the white slave traffic and of corrupting the German race with vile seductions. It has often been pointed

out that sexual envy seems to have motivated Hitler; certainly the Führer's enigmatic private life was a real puzzle for everyone but the Nazi propagandists, who held it up to the nation as a splendid example of selfless and blameless living.

With Julius Streicher, Nazi Jew-baiting hit rock bottom. A brute of a man, a sadist and pervert who loved to strut the streets of Nuremberg carrying a whip, Streicher peddled anti-Semitic filth to the nation in *Der Stürmer*. Its pages constantly featured warning cartoon strips of innocent blond German girls falling into the clutches of Jewish schoolteachers or doctors. The victims were invariably paragons of teutonic beauty, with blonde hair and blue eyes; the villains fat, swarthy, reeking of garlic, with thick lips, and a monstrous nose.

It was crude to the point of childishness – but the German people consistently looked the other way.

◁ ◁ *Menace: the S.S., Himmler's élite, parade through Berlin. It was one of Himmler's deputies, Hans Frank, who told his men that "I could not eliminate all lice and Jews in only one year. But in the course of time, and if you help me, this end will be attained."*
△ *Reply: the obvious counter-blast to the Nazi anti-Semitic programme. It was a simple truth, stated simply. But it could never aspire to the murderous glamour of the Nazi line.*

The Po is waiting for YOU

وریاے پو تمہارا انتظار کر رہا ہے

BEACH-HEAD

APRILIA — CISTERNA
VIA APPIA
ISOLA BELLA
CAMPO MORTO
ANZIO — NETTUNO

DEATH'S HEAD!

THE BEACH-HEAD

is going to be the big blow against the Germans.

Wasn't that the slogan when the Allied troops landed at Nettuno on January 21st?

TODAY

exactly three months of hard fighting have passed and you can now celebrate this event.

But it is still merely a beach-head, paved with the skulls of thousands of British and American soldiers!

The Beach-Head has become a Death's Head!

It is welcoming You with a grin, and also those who are coming after you across the sea for an appointment with death.

Do they know what they are in for?
Yes, they feel that they are landing on a

DEATH'S HEAD

AI - 065-4-44

Depressing the "D-day dodgers"

The campaign in Italy produced a splendid crop of propaganda. Once again it was the Germans who took the initiative, and their favourite topic was the slow crawl of the Allied advance.

The 8th Army – or the "D-Day dodgers", as they became known after ill-advised criticism back at home – found themselves on the receiving end of a series of telling propaganda leaflets. Some of these were parodies of tourist literature, extolling the natural beauties of Italy on one side and showing death waiting for all on the other. There is a typical example above. Others, like the Anzio leaflet opposite, made the most out of local setbacks and defeats suffered by the Allies.

Then there was "Axis Sally", who broadcast to the front-line troops. Unlike the chilling conviction of the "black" broadcasts of *Soldatensender Calais*, the "Axis Sally" broadcasts

failed. They had too high an entertainment value. After playing a record of dance music "to cheer up you poor boys in your cold trenches", "Sally" would then commiserate with the uncomfortable time they were having. She used a sultry, caressing tone which completely failed to achieve the desired effect; it sounded like a bad impersonation of Mae West and Marlene Dietrich combined, and the result was frankly comic.

Against heavy-handed blandishments of this kind, 8th Army morale held up well. The 8th Army had, by the time of the Italian campaign, evolved its own image. This was typified by the cartoonist Jon and his "Two Types" – hardened veteran officers from the days of the desert war, with desert boots, elaborately sloppy turn-out, and formidable R.A.F. handlebar moustaches.

As for the Americans in Italy, they had cartoon heroes of their own. These were the sloppy G.I.s "Willie and Joe", the creation of Bill Mauldin, which appeared in the American forces newspaper *Stars and Stripes*. Willie and Joe summed up the lot of the weary infantryman to whom no discomfort came as a real surprise. "I can't get no lower, Willie, my buttons is in the way" – or, sourly regarding a shot-torn village: "Let B Company go in first. They ain't been kissed yet."

The propaganda war in Italy therefore had its highlights, but little practical effect on either side. Despite the many setbacks encountered between Salerno and the final German surrender in the north, the Allies knew that they were winning the war. For their part, the Germans resisted every effort of the Allied propagandists. Kesselring's troops fought on undaunted to the end.

△ *A classic example of the German "perverted tourist" propaganda technique, used lavishly from Salerno until the end in Italy.*
◁◁ *How the Germans exploited the Allies' discomfiture in the Anzio beach-head.*

INDIA ARISE!

Encouraged by India's pre-war record of civil disobedience and demands for independence, the Japanese made many attempts to sabotage the war effort of British India by inducing the population to expel the British, and some very strong leaflets appeared. The Indian politician Subhas Chandra Bose became the figurehead of this movement abroad, first in Germany and then in Japan. He headed a skeletal Indian government-in-exile under Axis patronage and formed the "Indian National Army", recruited from Indian deserters and intended to fight beside the Japanese on the Burma front.

Although the Indian Congress refused to identify itself with the British warfare, and despite several disturbances within the country, India's response to the war was magnicent. Bose's "Indian National Army" only attracted a trickle of volunteers and never became a force to be reckoned with. Despite the strenuous efforts of the Japanese propagandists, India fought loyally for the Allied cause. In fact the country contributed the largest voluntary recruitment ever recorded in history: over two million by 1945. Even more important than the manpower contribution was India's economic aid, which made the country militarily self-sufficient and enabled her to supply the imperial armies in Africa and the Middle East. India emerged from the war as a creditor nation, ripe for independence. Her most serious problem was her internal differences—the very factor that the Japanese had tried in vain to exploit.

◁ Indians are urged to drive out Churchill, the British demon.
▷ △ and ▷ Attempts to canalise the independence movement and shake off British control.

Pleas for Co-Prosperity

There was always a note of naïveté about Japanese propaganda. It was reflected in the cosy title which the Japanese gave to their conquests in South-East Asia and the Pacific: the "South-East Asia Co-Prosperity Sphere", suggestive of a giant co-operative friendly society. It did not fit in with the brutal reality of Japanese military occupation. The trouble was that the reason for the sudden expansion of the Japanese Empire was painfully obvious: exploitation.

During the battle for the Philippines in 1941-42, the Japanese issued a crude, line-drawn leaflet showing a genial Japanese soldier giving a cigarette to a battered-looking Filipino soldier. In the background American troops can be seen running away, carrying a ripped and tattered American flag. "You are our pals," announced the legend. Our enemies are the Americans." Simple efforts such as this, and rhyming tags like the example below (more appropriate to a nursery school wall than an international propaganda campaign) had little chance. They certainly did not prevent the Filipino resistance movement from becoming one of the most powerful subversive elements in the entire "Co-Prosperity Sphere".

Primary education pamphlets were issued in Tokyo in series with titles like "The Schools Weekly, Primer Edition", and "The A.B.C. Weekly". A typical, run of the mill example read as follows:

"We have a new *Ministry*. It is the *Greater East Asia Ministry*.

"Mr. Kazuo Aoki is the *Minister* of the new Ministry."

Then, accompanying a photograph of prisoners from the "Doolittle Raid" on Tokyo: "Here you see some American *airmen*.

"They are the crew of the American planes which *raided* Japan on April 18.

"They have been *punished with heavy penalties.*

"The crew of any aircraft raiding Japan will be punished *with death.*"

An Anglo-Japanese translation key follows.

In general, Japan's propaganda efforts always retained the amateur look of a back-streets printer. They never made the most out of the formidable achievements born of the months of victory, or whipped up any effective anti-British feeling.

▽ *A pathetic attempt to justify Japan's "Runaway Victory" in the eyes of her victims. Even the Nazi boast of the "New Order in Europe" carried more conviction.*

Let us join hands !

Don't lose your lovely native lands

Trust not the sly Americans.

Come, join hands and help us build

A true home of our God sent East.

KEKOEATAN ASIA

HIMPOENLAH KERTAS APIAPI NO.111

◁ and ▽ *Match-box label propaganda was widely used by the Japanese. Colourfully printed, extolling Japanese military might, and ridiculing the British, Americans, and Chinese, they were sold "over the counter" and were often solemnly dropped on Allied airfields as well.*

A POSTMARK BETRAYED THIS H.Q...

USE THE **ARMY POST OFFICE**

Just how effective was the propaganda of World War II?

Webster's International Dictionary defines "propaganda" as "any systematic, widespread dissemination or promotion of particular ideas, doctrines, practices, etc., to further one's own cause or to damage an opposing one". And as far as war-time propaganda is concerned certain generalisations have to be considered.

First, propaganda of any kind has singularly little effect on the enemy when he happens to be winning. But this obvious fact is compounded by other factors. The Japanese were a case in point. The loyalty of their rank and file was proverbial; surrender or capture spelled unthinkable disgrace. Nothing proved this more clearly than the jungle fugitives on Guam in the Marianas islands who refused to accept that Japan had surrendered and held out against the day when the Japanese Army would return. These men continued to be rounded up long after 1945, one of them holding out until 1972. They belonged to an army which had been told that only torture and death awaited them at the hands of the Americans; but far more effective was the Japanese soldier's instinctive, unshakeable loyalty to his Emperor.

Similarly, German S.S. troops were also generally impervious to Allied propaganda, but this was not unique to the S.S. The best example was to be found in the Luftwaffe airborne units, which proved themselves tough and determined fighters from their early triumphs, right through the North African and Italian campaigns, with a fighting tradition and pride in their unit second to none.

The records show that only 59 British P.O.W.s responded to the call of the "Crusade Against Bolshevism" and enlisted in the *Waffen*-S.S. German recruiting propaganda had much greater success on the Eastern Front—but there the situation was different because of the wider array of minority nationalities: Latvians, Ukrainians, Cossacks, etc. In fact, one of the last actions of the war in Europe was a cavalry attack by a Cossack unit fighting with the Germans in northern Italy.

Awareness of victory, then, plus nationalist pride and military tradition, created a formidable shell for propaganda to crack. But – paradoxically – World War II produced plenty of cases where the reverse did not hold true in defeat. The population of besieged Warsaw in September 1939; the Finns during the "Winter War" of 1939-40; the British under the shadow of invasion and the perils of the Blitz in 1940; the endurance of the Leningraders during their 30-month siege: all were apparently hopeless situations in which propaganda appeals by the enemy had little or no effect.

The same applied to the fighting men. The British Guards held out at "Knightsbridge" in the Battle of Gazala–because they were the Guards. Four months later the Italo-German *Panzerarmee* and *Afrika Korps* fought on long after any reasonable hope of victory had evaporated. Similarly, the stand of the German paratroops at Cassino was later mirrored by that of the British 1st Airborne Division at Arnhem. And the hopeless defence of Iwo Jima in 1945 by General Kuribayashi's Japanese surpassed all these examples. While radio contact with Japan remained, Kuribayashi's messages reflected nothing but regret at having let the Americans establish themselves on Imperial Japanese territory.

It has often been claimed that the French collapse in 1940 was largely the result of months of eroding propaganda. There was certainly an intense propaganda campaign during the "Phoney War" while the French and German armies watched each other across the No-Man's Land between the Maginot and Siegfried Lines. Huge loudspeakers hurled messages backwards and forwards and leaflets were scattered lavishly. But on at least one occasion German attempts to sap the morale of the Maginot Line garrisons broke down in farce. A huge German placard appeared one morning, informing the French "Soldiers of the North" that their wives and girl friends were being unfaithful back home. The French troops at whom this was aimed riposted with a placard of their own: "We don't give a damn–we're from the south!" The truth of the matter is that the propaganda which did the most damage to French morale before the catastrophe of 1940 was not German, but Communist; Communist subversion and agitation had been rife in France long before the signing of the Nazi-Soviet Non-Aggression Pact of August 1939.

When all is said and done, propaganda aims at the mind; and war-time propaganda could be described as a form of mental tear gas to prevent the enemy from doing his job as effectively as he might otherwise have done. In war-time conditions, propaganda aimed at one's own population tends to pall after a while—people get tired of being exhorted. But it is nevertheless essential, for morale; a good parallel is the anti-aircraft barrage during the London Blitz. The damage done by the A.A. guns to the German bombers was negligible; but the Londoners found that air raids were far more bearable when they knew that their own guns were replying to the thunder of enemy bombs.

Conversely, the German people proved that even when the news is uniformly bad and official propaganda manifestly untrue, the general reaction is one of cynical humour, never of confusion and despair.

◁ ◁ *Familiar images used to ram home a principle of war-time security precautions.*

▽ *Simple, cartoon treatment– and an easy-to-remember rhyming slogan.*

TITTLE TATTLE LOST THE BATTLE

Like Napoleon, Hitler was a master of the big lie; and one of the biggest lies produced by the propaganda machine of the Third Reich was the "crusade against Bolshevism for the New Europe" line. Unfortunately this took some little time to emerge. Until 1940 Goebbels and his copywriters concentrated their efforts against individual victims–the Czechs, the Poles, the French, the British. Not until the invasion of Russia did the "crusade against Bolshevism" take shape. Once established, however, it remained–particularly when the Eastern Front began to be beaten back towards the Reich.

Joachim Peiper, the *Waffen-S.S.* commander who narrowly escaped hanging for his responsibility for the deliberate murder of American prisoners during the Battle of the Bulge in December 1944, was one among thousands who believed in the "New Europe" dream. Seven years after the end of the war, he wrote to his former comrades: "Don't forget that it was in the ranks of the S.S. that the first European died."

Here, for a certainty, Nazi propaganda had won a lasting victory . . .

▷ *An ever-recurring theme in German propaganda: the German soldier as the champion of European freedom.*

▽ *To win over Russians to the side of their German "liberators"–the horrors of Bolshevism compared with the brave new world for which the Third Reich was fighting the war.*

Deutschlands Sieg
EUROPAS FREIHEIT

БОЛЬШЕВИЗМ

НОВАЯ ЕВРОПА

CHAPTER 124
Assault from the East

In 1944 the Soviet summer offensive was to move forward successively over all sectors of the front from the Arctic tundra to the mouth of the Dniestr on the Black Sea. It can thus be compared in extent to Hitler's Operation "Barbarossa" begun three years before. Now the situation was reversed.

In addition to the will to destroy the armed forces of Germany and her satellites, the U.S.S.R. also had territorial and political ambitions: to impose a dictated peace on Finland; to bring Estonia, Latvia, and Lithuania back under Soviet rule; to install a puppet government in Poland; and to prepare to take over Rumania, Bulgaria, Hungary, and Yugoslavia.

Stalin, the head of the Soviet Government and Secretary General of the Soviet Communist Party, was therefore going beyond the popular Clausewitzian view of a purely military conception of strategy and adopting the principles formerly laid down by Lenin: "War is essentially a political fact . . . war is one part of a whole: that whole is politics", and by Frunze, the creator of the Red Army:

▽ *Red Army infantry advance over somewhat meagre German barbed wire defences. With ever-improving co-operation between Soviet infantry, armour, and aircraft, the Red Army was more than a match for the German Army, for all its skill in defensive fighting.*

△ *Soviet soldiers inspect a ruined Finnish emplacement on the road to Viipuri, or Vyborg as it was known to the Russians. As in the Winter War of 1939-40, the Russians attacked across the Karelian isthmus in overwhelming numerical and matériel superiority, but this time the advantage of strength was matched by the skill with which it was used.*

△▷ *Russian gunners on the Hangö peninsula, ceded to Russia by Finland after the Winter War.*

▽▷ *Russian armour on the move through Karelia. The Finns resisted brilliantly, but this time even the weather was against them.*

"Questions of military strategy and political and economic strategy are closely inter-related and form a coherent whole."

This is clearly opposed to the American military doctrine which Eisenhower obeyed in early April 1945 when he stopped his 12th Army Group on the Elbe at Magdeburg, since Berlin no longer had any importance militarily. There have, it is true, been many cases in which military operations have been gravely compromised by political interference.

Stavka's resources

In view of the failing strength of the Wehrmacht, Stalin could well afford to depart from the long-established principles of pure strategy. In effect, early in the summer of 1944 *Stavka* had 500 infantry and 40 artillery divisions, and 300 armoured or mechanised brigades with over 9,000 tanks, supported by 16,600 fighters, fighter-bombers, and twin-engined bombers, whilst behind the front the effort put into training, organisation, and industrial production in 1943 was kept up at the same rate in 1944. It should also be emphasised that the Red

Army's conduct of operations was now more relaxed. A judicious series of promotions had brought to the top of the major units many exceptionally able commanders. Stalin and *Stavka* allowed them an easier rein than in the past, whereas their enemy was being deprived of all initiative by the despot of Berchtesgaden.

First offensive: Finland

The first blows of the Soviet summer offensive fell on Finland. As we have seen, thanks to the Swedish Government's action as an intermediary, negotiations were on the point of being concluded between Helsinki and Moscow in the late winter, and the Finns were no longer insisting on the return to the *status quo* of March 1940. The talks fell through, however, because Moscow demanded from this small unhappy country an indemnity of 600 million dollars' worth of raw materials and goods, spread over the next five years.

When spring came, the situation of Finland and her valiant army could hardly give rise to optimism. The defeat

of Field-Marshal von Küchler and the German Army Group "North", driven from the banks of the Neva to those of the Narva, deprived Marshal Mannerheim of any hope of German help in the event of a Soviet offensive.

Mannerheim had therefore divided the bulk of his forces in two: in the isthmus between the Gulf of Finland and Lake Ladoga he had put six divisions, including his 1st Armoured Division, and two brigades, all under III and IV Corps; on the front of the river Svir', which runs from Lake Onega to Lake Ladoga, he had nine divisions and three brigades. This was a lot, to be sure but, Mannerheim wrote:

"A reduction of the troops in East Karelia would, however, constitute a surrender of this strategically valuable area and be a good bargaining-point for the attainment of peace. The disposition of the troops was also based on the not unreasonable hope that the fortifications of the Isthmus would compensate for the weakness of man-power."

The Finnish III and IV Corps could in fact count on three successive lines of fortifications, the first two from 44 to 50 miles long and the third 75 miles.

This was small stuff against the powerful forces massed by the Russians, especially in artillery, for the Leningrad Front, still under the command of General L. A. Govorov. Finnish Intelligence sources revealed that the Russians put some 20 infantry divisions on the Finnish front, together with four armoured brigades, five or six tank regiments, and four regiments of assault guns, that is some 450 armoured vehicles in all, and about 1,000 aircraft. For their part the official Soviet sources give no figures, so that we are inclined to believe the Finns. Silence implies consent.

Karelia overrun

On June 9 the Leningrad Front went over to the attack, with an artillery barrage of up to 250 guns per mile. Lieutenant-General D. N. Gussev and his 21st Army had been given the main task and this developed over a ten-mile front along the coastal sector, which allowed the Red Navy's Baltic Fleet to take part under the command of Admiral V. F. Tributs.

Mannerheim wrote: "June 10th may

△ ◁ Russian 122-mm howitzers
in action. The 122-mm howitzer,
an excellent weapon, was
introduced in 1938, and could
fire a 48-lb shell up to 12,900
yards. At a weight of only 2.2
tons, the weapon was easy to
move, clearly a factor of
considerable importance in the
swift Russian advances in the
second half of the war.
◁ ◁ Improvised observation post
in the forests of Karelia.
△ The standard but effective
Russian pattern of assault:
tanks and infantry.
◁ Soviet mortar crew provides
front line punch.

The Russian Yakovlev Yak-1 fighter and fighter-bomber

Engine: one Klimov M-105PA inline, 1,100-hp.
Armament: one 20-mm ShVAK cannon with 120 rounds and two 7.62-mm ShKAS machine guns with 375 rounds per gun, plus six RS-82 rockets.
Speed: 364 mph at 16,400 feet.
Climb: 4 minutes 30 seconds to 16,400 feet.
Ceiling: 32,800 feet.
Range: 435 miles.
Weight empty/loaded: 5,137/6,217 lbs.
Span: 32 feet 9¾ inches.
Length: 27 feet 9¾ inches.
Height: 8 feet 8 inches.

The Russian Petlyakov Pe-8 heavy bomber

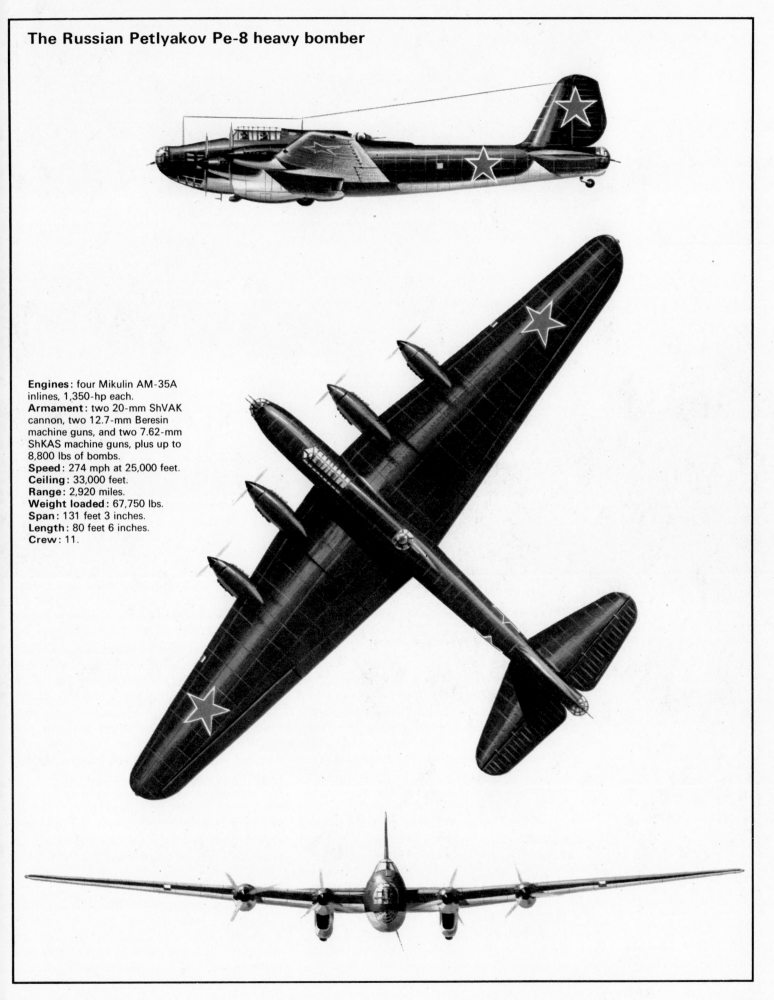

Engines: four Mikulin AM-35A inlines, 1,350-hp each.
Armament: two 20-mm ShVAK cannon, two 12.7-mm Beresin machine guns, and two 7.62-mm ShKAS machine guns, plus up to 8,800 lbs of bombs.
Speed: 274 mph at 25,000 feet.
Ceiling: 33,000 feet.
Range: 2,920 miles.
Weight loaded: 67,750 lbs.
Span: 131 feet 3 inches.
Length: 80 feet 6 inches.
Crew: 11.

▷ Safe from the prying eyes of Axis aircraft: a Russian tank turret dug in as a strongpoint on the Karelian front.

△ Women of Petrosavodsk on the Karelian front greet Major-General Kupryanon with light refreshments.

with reason be described as the black day of our war history. The infantry assault, carried out by three divisions of the Guards against a single Finnish regiment, broke the defence and forced the front in the coastal sector back about six miles. Furious fighting raged at a number of holding lines, but the on-storming massed armour broke their resistance.

"Because of the enemy's rapid advance, the 10th Division fighting on the coast sector lost most of its artillery. On June 11th, its cut-up units were withdrawn behind the V.T. (Vammelsuu-Taipale) position to be brought up to strength."

But hardly had the defenders of the isthmus taken up their positions than they were driven back by an attack which broke through north of the Leningrad–Viipuri (Vyborg) railway. The 1st Armoured Division counter-attacked, but

to no avail. Faced with this rapidly deteriorating situation, Mannerheim left the defence of the isthmus to General Oesch and ordered the evacuation of Karelia. This enabled him to pull out four divisions. Before there could be any reployment in force in the threatened sector, the Russian 21st Army made a fresh breakthrough and seized Viipuri on June 20.

What would have happened to the defence if the armies of the Karelian Front (General K. A. Meretskov) had come into battle on the same day as the Leningrad Front and had trapped the Finnish V and VI Corps between Lakes Ladoga and Onega? For unknown reasons the Russians only started their attack five or six days after Mannerheim had ordered the defenders to break off contact.

The Russian offensive in eastern Karelia took the form of a pincer movement. One army crossed the Svir' and pushed northwards to meet the other which, having forced the Masselskaya defile, exploited this success southwards. But the pincers closed on a vacuum and at the beginning of July the Finns, though reduced to four divisions, had nevertheless succeeded in re-establishing their positions on a pre-arranged line from Lake Ladoga on their right to Lake Loymola on their left, some 45 miles from the present Soviet-Finnish frontier.

Between Lake Ladoga and the Gulf of Finland, Govorov had a few more successes, in particular establishing a bridgehead on the north bank of the Vuoksa, along which ran the third defen-

△ Russian troops in "liberated" Viipuri.

sive position between Viipuri and Taipale. But finally everything quietened down and about July 15 General Oesch was able to state that the enemy forces opposite him were considerably thinner on the ground.

It would certainly be absurd to deny that the Red Army had won. The Finns had been driven back to their last line of defence and had lost the Karelia area, which they had intended to use as a counter in the forthcoming peace negotiations. The Soviet Union had also got the use of the Leningrad–Murmansk railway and canal which the Finns had begun in 1941.

In spite of the defeat, however, the fighting spirit of the Finish Army lived on. It counter-attacked incessantly and in the whole campaign very few Finns were taken prisoners. On balance Moscow seems to have realised that to wipe out the Finnish Army would have cost more than the literal submission of Helsinki to the March 1940 conditions was worth.

Time to get out

As we can see, Mannerheim had played the cards of dissuasion well. But, like his government, he agreed that the time had come for Finland to get out of the war. During the battle, instead of the six divisions for which he had asked O.K.H., he had got only one, the 129th, and a brigade of 80 assault guns. All the assurances, intermingled with threats,

proffered by Ribbentrop to President Ryti could not make up the difference. The day after Viipuri fell, and with it Finland's hopes, the Wehrmacht was suffering in Russia one of the bloodiest defeats in the history of the German Army, including Jena and Stalingrad.

On June 28, when he rejoined the German 20th Army fighting north of the Arctic Circle, Colonel-General Rendulic wrote of the impression Mannerheim made on him at their first meeting: "In spite of the prudence which he continually showed in official declarations, his words had an unmistakably pessimistic ring." This goes to show that the 76-year old Marshal saw further than Rendulic.

▽ Soviet troops move up towards the front through Viipuri. Note the large number of anti-tank rifles in evidence.

△ *A formation of Petlyakov Pe-2 light bomber and general purpose aircraft. One of the best machines of the war, the Pe-2 was pressed into service in a multitude of rôles.*

▷ *T-34 tanks with their infantry riders.*

Second offensive: Polotsk and the Pripet

On June 22, 1944, as if to celebrate the third anniversary of the German aggression, Stalin launched a large offensive operation between the Polotsk area and the north bank of the Pripet. This brought into action Bagramyan's 1st Baltic Front, Chernyakhovsky's 3rd Belorussian Front, Zakharov's 2nd Belorussian Front, and Rokossovsky's 1st Belorussian Front.

According to the *Great Patriotic War,* which we quote in Alexander Werth's version, the following were engaged in this offensive, including reserves: 166 infantry divisions, 31,000 guns and mortars, 5,200 tanks and self-propelled guns, and 6,000 aircraft. The Red Army had never before achieved such a concentration of force or had such huge quantities of supporting *matériel,* which included 25,000 two-ton lorries.

Michel Garder gives a lively account of the atmosphere of the Soviet summer offensive in his book *A War Unlike The Others.* He says:

"The patient work of the Red Army's general staff, which had prepared in great detail the grand plan of *Stavka,* resulted in this fantastic cavalcade. This was the true revenge for the summer of 1941! In the burning-hot July sky the Red Air Force was unopposed. White with dust the T-34's drove on westwards, breaking through the hedges, crushing down thickets, spitting out flame . . . with clusters of infantry clinging on to their rear platforms, adventure-bound. Swarms of men on motor-cycles . . . shouting cavalry . . . infantry in lorries . . . rocket-artillery cluttering up the road . . . the tracks . . . the paths . . . mowing down everything in their way.

"This was a long way from the stereotyped image of 'dejected troops herded to slaughter by Jewish political commissars'."

Marshal Vasilevsky had been sent to

Marshal Ivan Danielovich Chernyakhovsky was born in 1908 in the Ukraine, and entered the army via the Artillery Military School. In 1940 he was a captain in an armoured division, and distinguished himself at Yelna and Voronezh. As a brigadier he took Kursk in February 1943 and then held it during *"Zitadelle"*. With further promotion he took Ternopol' in spring 1944 and then received command of the 3rd Belorussian Front. He was killed on February 28, 1945.

Bagramyan and Chernyakhovsky as *Stavka*'s representative to co-ordinate their operations. Zhukov performed the same function with Zakharov and Rokossovsky.

The objective of the Soviet offensive was the destruction of Army Group "Centre", then commanded by Field-Marshal Busch, who in the early days of 1944 had taken over from Kluge at the latter's H.Q. at Minsk. Busch had four armies deployed from north to south as follows:

1. 3rd *Panzerarmee* (Colonel-General Reinhardt)
2. 4th Army (General von Tippelskirch)
3. 9th Army (General Jordan)
4. 2nd Army (Colonel-General Weiss)

By the end of the winter the withdrawals forced upon Army Groups "North" and "South" by the Soviet winter offensives had left Army Group "Centre" in a salient: the fortified area of Vitebsk on the Dvina was two-thirds encircled, whereas south of the Pripet Marshes Rokossovsky had got as far as the approaches to Kovel'. To counteract the threat to Field-Marshal Model's left at the end of March, Busch had been asked to send him eight divisions, including two Panzer.

Russian superiority in tanks and aircraft

When the Soviet summer offensive started, Army Group "Centre" was thus reduced to 37 divisions. On June 22 the 2nd Army was not attacked, and so the initial clash in the battle for Belorussia was between 166 Soviet and 28 German divisions, on a front extending over 435 miles. The Russian divisions had about 10,000 men. Those of Generals Jordan, Tippelskirch, and Reinhardt were very much under-strength, as can be seen in the account given by Major-General Heidkämper, chief-of-staff of the 3rd *Panzerarmee*. He showed that the Vitebsk salient was being held by LIII Corps along a front of 55 miles with the 206th, 4th and 6th Luftwaffe, and 246th Divisions, with 8,123 rifles (about 150 rifles per mile). Reserves consisted of a battalion of heavy artillery, two heavy anti-tank companies, and one Luftwaffe special service battalion. Colonel-General Reinhardt's VI and IX Corps were no better off, nor were the

4th and 9th Armies. German dispositions between the Pripet and the Dvina were thus as thin as a spider's web.

The mobile reserves which were to slow down then stop the onslaught of 4,500 Soviet tanks consisted of only the 20th Panzer and the 18th, 25th, and 60th *Panzergrenadier* Divisions with 400 tracked vehicles between them. For good measure add the same number of assault guns, and it will be seen that in armour the Germans were outnumbered by 5.6 to 1.

It was the same in the air: *Luftflotte* VI could get only an insignificant number of planes off the ground.

"Fortified areas"

The situation of Army Group "Centre" was such that if the enemy unleashed against it an attack of any strength it

◁ *German artillerymen prepare to reload their gun. Despite all their efforts, however, the out-numbered Germans could not stem the Russian advance.*
△ *The proof: German dead in the wake of the 2nd Belorussian Front's triumphant progress.*

could not expect to hold it. Again Hitler was to intervene and make Stalin's task easier. Firstly he laid down, in an order dated March 8, 1944, the building on the Eastern Front of a number of "fortified areas" to take over the rôles of the former fortresses. "Their task," his *Führerbefehl* of that day ordered, "is to prevent the enemy from seizing centres of decisive strategic importance. They are to allow themselves to be encircled so as to engage as many of the enemy as possible. They are to create opportunities for fruitful counter-attacks."

Controlled by an army group or army, the strongpoint garrison had instructions to hold out to the last man and no one except the Führer, acting on information from the army group commander, had the right to order withdrawal.

In the Army Group "Centre" sector nine towns were to be made fortified areas. These included Bobruysk on the Berezina, Mogilev and Orsha on the Dniepr, and Vitebsk on the Dvina. The troops manning these new areas were to be taken from the armies in the field, which their commanders regarded as a heresy.

Reinhardt made repeated objections to Hitler's orders, transmitted to him through Field-Marshal Busch, to shut away LIII Corps (General Gollwitzer) and three divisions in the so-called "fortified area" of Vitebsk. In the event of an attack in this sector the absence of these units would open up a breach which could not possibly be stopped, and enemy armour would thus pour through. Reinhardt even went to Minsk to state his case and was told sharply on April 21:

"Vitebsk's value is as a fortified area and the Führer will not change this point of view at any price. His opinion is that Vitebsk can engage between 30 and 40 enemy divisions which would otherwise be free to attack west and south west," then: "It is also a matter of prestige. Vitebsk is the only place on the Eastern Front whose loss would resound throughout the world."

Reinhardt was dismissed in these terms; neither Tippelskirch nor Jordan were any better received by Busch. Jordan, who on the following May 20 proposed to Hitler that if it were to appear likely that the Soviets would launch an offensive in Belorussia, the Germans should withdraw to the Dniepr and the Berezina, thus shortening their line from 435 to 280 miles, was summarily dismissed with

"Another of those generals perpetually looking backwards".

Hitler misunderstands Soviet intentions

It is true that the Führer did not consider that Army Group "Centre" would be the immediate objective of the offensive which, he admitted, the enemy would launch as soon as the ground was sufficiently hard again. In all evidence it was Army Groups "North Ukraine" and "South Ukraine" which were threatened, as Stalin clearly had his eyes fixed on the Rumanian capital and the Ploieşti oil-fields, then the Balkan peninsula and the Turkish narrows, the age-old goal of Imperial Russia, not to mention Budapest and the rich Hungarian plains.

From early June onwards reports from the front, based on direct information, on aerial reconnaissance by the Luftwaffe, on the interception and analysis of radio messages, and on the interrogation of prisoners and deserters, all seemed to indicate the progressive build-up of a powerful assault force between the Pripet and the Dvina. In particular the Red Air Force was growing steadily in numbers every day. When Major-General Gehlen, head of Section East of O.K.H. Intelligence, told Hitler about all this, the Führer retorted that it was merely a clumsy decoy movement. Stalin wanted the Germans to bring over from Moldavia to Belorussia the forces they were holding opposite the true centre of gravity of Russian strategy, but Hitler was not going to fall into that trap.

This opinion was so fixed in his mind that during the night of June 24-25 he obstinately refused to yield to the despair of his closest collaborators, who entreated him to agree to the measures which had become necessary consequent upon the collapse of the 3rd *Panzerarmee* in the Vitebsk sector, whilst at the confluence of the Dniepr and the Berezina the 9th Army had reached the limits of endurance under ever increasing attacks. There was an eye-witness to these events.

Colonel-General Dr. Lothar Rendulic was at the Berghof that evening, having been summoned there urgently to be given command of the German 20th Army (Lappland) after the accidental death of Colonel-General Dietl. In his memoirs Rendulic says:

"Hitler thought that the main Soviet effort was developing in the south and considered that these Russian attacks east of Warsaw were mere demonstrations. It was a notable miscalculation, as events were to show. He forbade any reserves to be taken from the south and moved to Warsaw. I can say here that when I came out of the conference I asked Colonel-General Jodl how he could let this appreciation of the situation go unchallenged. He replied: 'We fought the Führer for two whole days, then when he ran out of arguments he said: "Leave me. I am relying on my intuition." What can you do in a situation like that?'"

During the night of June 19–20 the 240,000 partisans who controlled the forests in Belorussia cut the lines of communication of Army Group "Centre" in more than 10,000 places as far west as

△ ◁ *Russian infantry double over a pontoon bridge across the River Bug, another major river barrier overcome.*
◁ ◁ *Germans struggle to extricate a sidecar combination during the retreat from Vitebsk.*
▽ ◁ *The same problem for horsed transport.*

△ *The promise that was wearing thin: the German Army staving off the Red flood from Poland's agricultural areas.*
◁ *Albert Speer, wearing an Organisation "Todt" brassard, in conversation with Major Dr. Kupfer. Upon Speer's department fell most of the work involved in throwing up Germany's eastern ramparts.*

Minsk. At dawn on the 22nd the forces of the 1st Baltic and the 3rd Belorussian Fronts went over to the attack on both sides of Vitebsk. The 1st Belorussian Front went into action on the following day. Generals Bagramyan and Chernyakhovsky had been given as their first objective the capture of Vitebsk by a pincer movement, which would give their comrade Rokossovsky the time to pierce the German 9th Army's positions in the area of Bobruysk. When both these results had been achieved the two Belorussian Fronts would let loose their armoured formations, which would converge in the direction of Minsk. A second pincer would thus be formed and this would crush Army Group "Centre". Bagramyan and Chernyakhovsky took just 48 hours to overpower the resistance of the 3rd *Panzerarmee* north-west and south-east of Vitebsk. During this brief spell the German commander also used up his meagre reserves as well as the 14th Division, sent to him by Busch as a reinforcement. Busch could ill afford the loss. In particular the German right wing, which consisted of VI Corps (General Pfeiffer, killed in this action), collapsed completely under the impact of the Soviet 5th Army and four armoured brigades, whose attack was preceded and supported by V Artillery Corps (520

◁ *The inhabitants of the Minsk area left behind by the Germans greet the liberating Russian forces.*
▽ *Ground crew at work on Lavochkin fighters on a forward airfield. Note the Russian-built "Dakota" landing. By 1944 the Red Air Force's disasters of 1941 and 1942 were no more than evil memories. Its squadrons now had good equipment and enjoyed total superiority over the Luftwaffe.*

heavy guns) and tactical air formations acting with a strength, a spirit, and an accuracy hitherto unknown on the Eastern Front.

No retreat from Vitebsk

At 1520 hours on June 24 Zeitzler called Reinhardt from the Berghof to ask if he considered the mission assigned to him at the fortified area of Vitebsk to be vital. The army commander, according to his chief-of-staff, replied candidly that "LIII Corps was surrounded, though still only

△ *Scorched earth again.*
△▷ *Russian infantry pour over a partially demolished bridge. The infantry could then secure a bridgehead and allow the engineers to throw up a bridge for the tanks to cross.*
▽▷ *German demolition in Vitebsk.*

▽ *A Russian poster warns of the reception German aircraft will receive. But by the middle of 1944 the few aircraft that the Luftwaffe could still muster were wholly on the defensive.*

weakly; that this was the moment to order him to try to break out; that every quarter of an hour the Russian ring to the west of Vitebsk was thickening."

When Zeitzler remarked that the Führer feared heavy losses in supplies of all kinds if the fortified area were to be abandoned hastily, Reinhardt burst out: "If the ring closes we shall lose not only supplies and ammunition, but the whole of LIII Corps with its five divisions." As usual nothing came of these remonstrations, for at 1528 hours Zeitzler came back from seeing Hitler and informed Reinhardt: "The Führer has decided that Vitebsk will be held." According to Major-General Heidkämper, Reinhardt stood "petrified" at the news.

At 1830 hours, however, the incompetent despot agreed to some relaxation of this grotesque order and signalled 3rd *Panzerarmee*: "LIII Corps will leave one division to garrison Vitebsk and break out westwards to rejoin our lines. Report name of commander of this division. Swear him in by radio as new commander of 'Vitebsk fortified area'. Make him confirm his oath."

This order was no less absurd than the one which went before it. The 206th Division (Lieutenant-General Hitter) was nominated. To this unit alone was entrusted the defence of positions prepared for four divisions. And it was too late. LIII Corps was intercepted and crushed during its retreat and when its commander, General Gollwitzer, surrendered to the

Russians on June 27 he had only 200 of his men with him and of these 180 were wounded. The worst had happened: the destruction of Vitebsk opened a breach in the German line more than 28 miles wide. Reinhardt was now reduced to three worn-out divisions and 70 guns. Nothing and nobody could now stop the thrustful Chernyakhovsky from driving on along the Lepel'–Minsk axis with the 5th Guards Army under Marshal of Armoured Forces Pavel A. Rotmistrov.

Rokossovsky takes Bobruysk

Further south on the Belorussian front, the same causes could only produce the same effects and General Jordan, C.-in-C. 9th Army, was no luckier than Reinhardt; XXXV Corps, defending the fortified area of Bobruysk with four divisions, suffered the same fate as LIII Corps. When he opened his offensive on June 24, General Rokossovsky had taken good care not to launch his 1st Belorussian Front forces against the German fortified areas, but to push them into gaps north and south of the River Berezina. Three days of hard fighting brought him victory. South of Bobruysk he overcame XLI Panzer Corps (Lieutenant-General Hoffmeister) and cut off the retreating XXXV Corps (Lieutenant-General von Lützow), leaving

it trapped in the fortified area.

On June 29 16,000 Germans emerged from the pocket and gave themselves up, leaving behind them the bodies of 18,000 of their comrades. By now the mounted, motorised, mechanised, and armoured forces of General Pliev, one of the most brilliant cavalry commanders of the war, had reached Ossipovichi, some eight miles south-east of Minsk, and were rumbling forward to meet the 5th Guards Tank Army, which had passed Lepel' and was now in Borisov.

The situation of the German 4th Army, now at grips with greatly superior forces on the 2nd Belorussian Front, was scarcely any better. Faced with disasters on his right and left, General von Tippelskirch, now in command *vice* Colonel-General Heinrici, had to use all his initiative to get his army out of its positions along the river Proina and back to the Dniepr. The fortified areas of Mogilev and Orsha on the Dniepr, however, were soon overcome by Zakharov and Chernyakhovsky, and became the graveyards respectively of the 6th (Lieutenant-General Henie) and the 12th (Lieutenant-General Wagner) Divisions.

Tippelskirch thus had to continue his retreat westwards across rough forest land infested with marches and, particularly, thick with partisans. It is no wonder that, as planned by *Stavka,* Rotmistrov and Pliev got to Minsk before him on July 3, joining forces behind his back and condemning his XII and XXVII

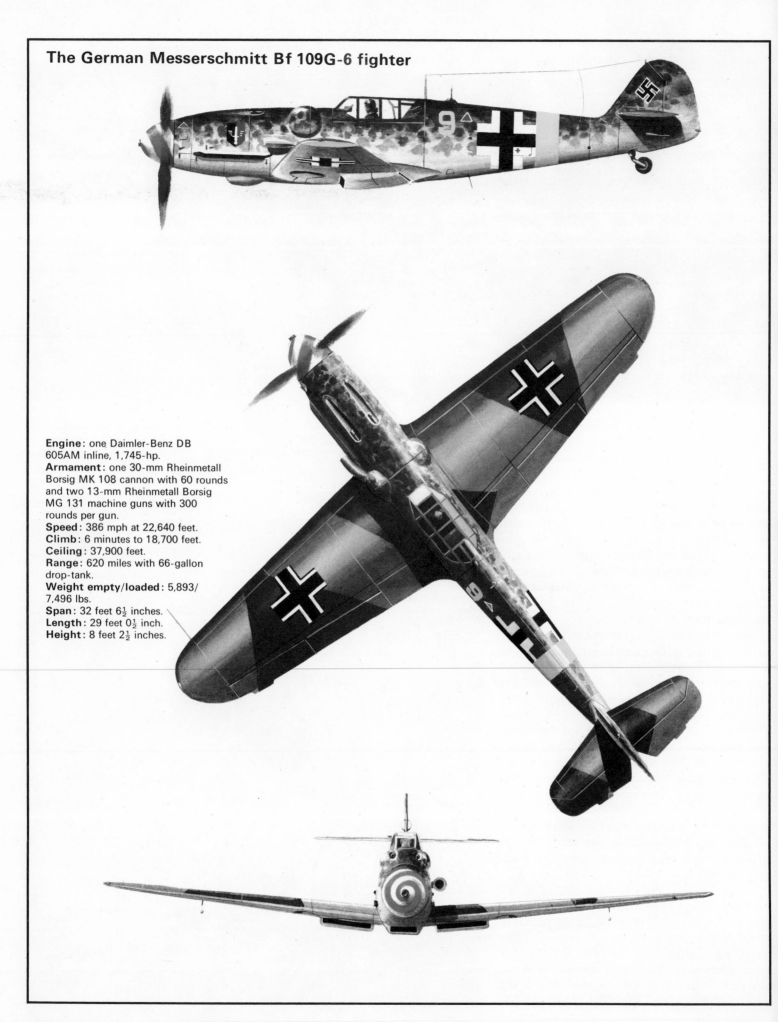

The German Messerschmitt Bf 109G-6 fighter

Engine: one Daimler-Benz DB 605AM inline, 1,745-hp.
Armament: one 30-mm Rheinmetall Borsig MK 108 cannon with 60 rounds and two 13-mm Rheinmetall Borsig MG 131 machine guns with 300 rounds per gun.
Speed: 386 mph at 22,640 feet.
Climb: 6 minutes to 18,700 feet.
Ceiling: 37,900 feet.
Range: 620 miles with 66-gallon drop-tank.
Weight empty/loaded: 5,893/ 7,496 lbs.
Span: 32 feet 6½ inches.
Length: 29 feet 0½ inch.
Height: 8 feet 2½ inches.

The Russian Yakovlev Yak-9D fighter

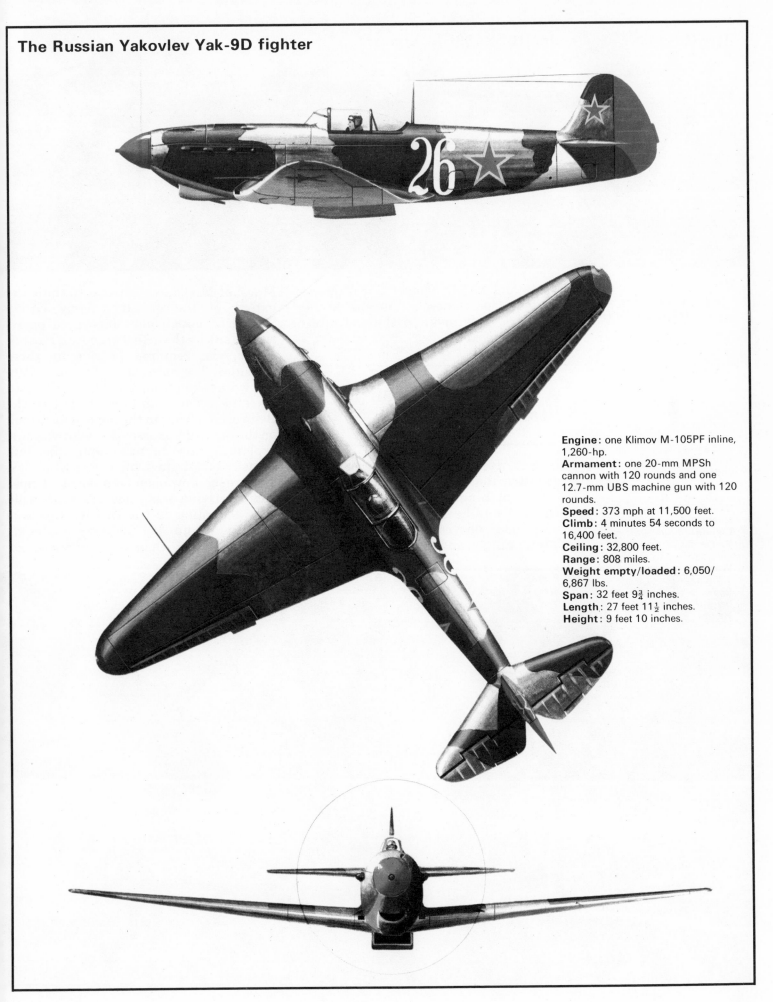

Engine: one Klimov M-105PF inline, 1,260-hp.
Armament: one 20-mm MPSh cannon with 120 rounds and one 12.7-mm UBS machine gun with 120 rounds.
Speed: 373 mph at 11,500 feet.
Climb: 4 minutes 54 seconds to 16,400 feet.
Ceiling: 32,800 feet.
Range: 808 miles.
Weight empty/loaded: 6,050/6,867 lbs.
Span: 32 feet $9\frac{3}{4}$ inches.
Length: 27 feet $11\frac{1}{2}$ inches.
Height: 9 feet 10 inches.

Corps and XXXIX Panzer Corps (respectively under Generals Vincenz Müller, Voelkers, Martinek) to the sad fate of "moving pockets".

A defeat worse than Stalingrad

It was June 28 before Hitler finally admitted that the Belorussian offensive was something more than a diversion. On that day he sacked General Busch, who had obeyed his directives unquestioningly, and replaced him by Field-

Marshal Model, who strove to limit the extent of the disaster. Army Group "North", though now uncovered on its right flank by the defeat of the 3rd *Panzerarmee,* was required to give up three divisions. Ten more, including four Panzer, were taken from Army Group "North Ukraine". These units were sent to the Belorussian front in the hope of an attack on the flank of Rokossovsky, who was now exploiting his victory along the line Minsk – Baranovichi – Brest-Litovsk. The breach now open between the Pripet and the Dvina was some 185 miles wide and, according to the O.K.H., this was swallowing up 126 infantry divisions and no fewer than 62 armoured or

△ *The inevitable result: a German armoured column destroyed by Russian artillery and aircraft.*

▷ *German prisoners walk back to a collection point in the rear, past a less fortunate compatriot.*
▽ *A German soldier lies by an abandoned* leichte Feldhaubitze *18/40 of 10.5-cm calibre.*
△▷ *Civilians freed from a Nazi camp near Minsk begin their journey home.*
▽▷ *Some of the 57,600 German prisoners taken by the Belorussian Fronts wait to be paraded through Moscow.*

mechanised brigades with at least 2,500 tanks. On July 8 the last "moving pocket" surrendered behind the Russian lines with 17,000 men, having run out of ammunition. Out of 37 divisions in Army Group "Centre" on the previous June 22, 28 had been badly mauled, if not actually cut to pieces, and an enormous mass of *matériel,* including 215 tanks and more than 1,300 guns, had been captured.

According to statistics from Moscow, which appear reliable, the Germans lost between these two dates some 285,000 dead and prisoners, including 19 corps and divisional commanders. The Belorussian disaster was thus worse than Stalingrad and all the more so since, when Paulus resigned himself to the inevitable, the "Second Front" was still only a distant threat to the Third Reich.

Stalin celebrated in true Roman style by marching seemingly endless columns of 57,600 prisoners-of-war through the streets of Moscow with their generals at the head. Alexander Werth, the *Sunday Times* correspondent, was there and he described the behaviour of the Russian crowd as the men passed by:

"Youngsters booed and whistled, and even threw things at the Germans, only to be immediately restrained by the adults; men looked on grimly and in silence; but many women, especially elderly women, were full of commiseration (some even had tears in their eyes) as they looked at these bedraggled 'Fritzes'. I remember one old woman murmuring 'just like our poor boys . . . tozhe pognali ne voinu (also driven into war)'."

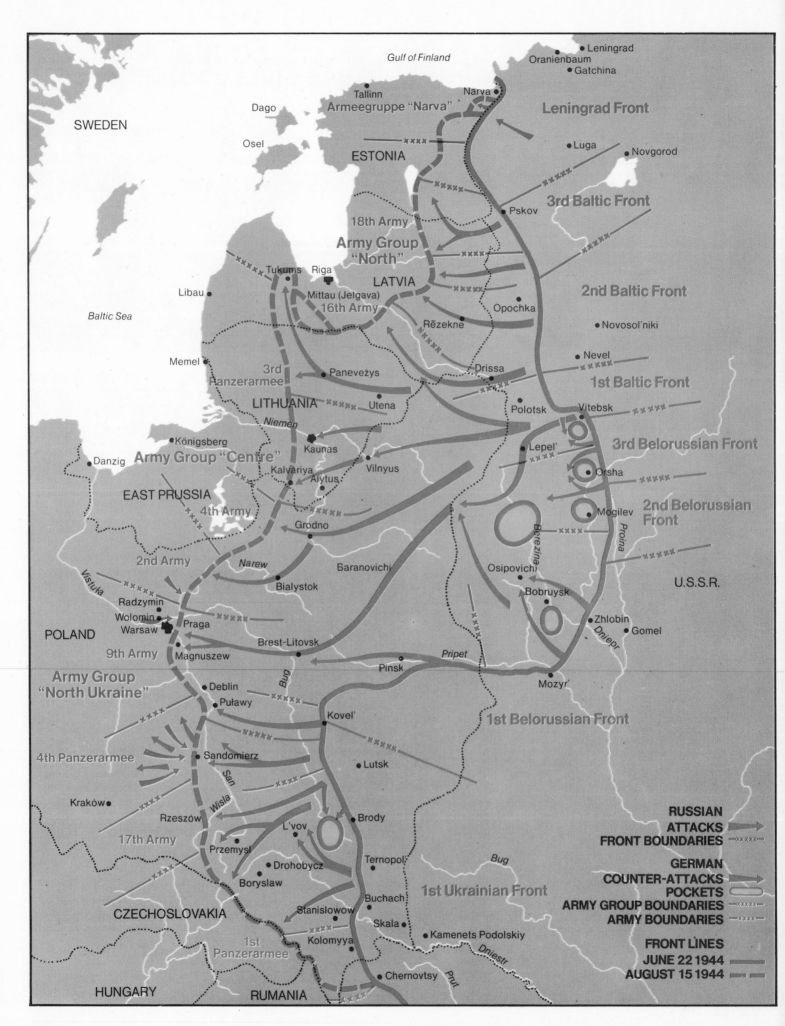

SWEDEN

Gulf of Finland

Leningrad
Oranienbaum
Gatchina

Dago

Osel

Tallinn
Armeegruppe "Narva"
Narva

Leningrad Front

ESTONIA

Luga
Novgorod

Pskov

3rd Baltic Front

18th Army
Army Group
"North"

Tukums
Riga

Mittau (Jelgava)
16th Army

2nd Baltic Front

Libau

Opochka

Baltic Sea

Rēzekne

Novosol'niki

Memel

3rd
Panzerarmee

Panevežys

Drissa

Nevel

1st Baltic Front

LITHUANIA

Utena

Polotsk

Vitebsk

Niemen

Königsberg

Kaunas

Lepel'

3rd Belorussian Front

Danzig

Army Group "Centre"

Kalvariya
Alytus

Vilnyus

Orsha

2nd Belorussian
Front

EAST PRUSSIA

4th Army

Mogilev

Grodno

Proina

2nd Army

Narew

Baranovichi

Osipovichi

Berezina

U.S.S.R.

Bialystok

Bobruysk

Vistula

Zhlobin

Radzymin
Wolomin
Warsaw

Praga

Dniepr

Gomel

POLAND

Brest-Litovsk

9th Army

Magnuszew

Pinsk

Pripet

Mozyr'

Army Group
"North Ukraine"

Deblin

Puławy

Bug

1st Belorussian Front

Kovel'

4th Panzerarmee

Sandomierz

San

Lutsk

Kraków

Wisla

Brody

Rzeszów

17th Army

Przemysl

L'vov

Ternopol

Bug

Drohobycz

Boryslaw

Buchach

1st Ukrainian Front

CZECHOSLOVAKIA

Stanislowow

Skala

Kolomyya

Kamenets Podolskiy

1st
Panzerarmee

Dniestr

Chernovtsy

Prut

HUNGARY

RUMANIA

RUSSIAN
ATTACKS
FRONT BOUNDARIES

GERMAN
COUNTER-ATTACKS
POCKETS
ARMY GROUP BOUNDARIES
ARMY BOUNDARIES

FRONT LINES
JUNE 22 1944
AUGUST 15 1944

1792

CHAPTER 125
On to the Vistula

Stalin gave Bagramyan, Chernyakhovsky, Zakharov, and Rokossovsky the job of exploiting as deeply and as fast as possible the victory at Minsk, the extent of which, thanks to Hitler, seems to have exceeded even *Stavka*'s highest hopes.

Under the terms of the new directives, the forces of the 1st Baltic Front were given as their objective the Gulf of Riga, whilst the three Belorussian Fronts would move first on to the line Kaunas–Grodno –Brest-Litovsk, then force their way across the Niemen and the Bug, as they had done over the Dniepr and the Berezina. Colonel-General Chernyakhovsky would then take on the defences of eastern Prussia, whilst Zakharov and Rokossovsky (the latter just having been promoted Marshal of the U.S.S.R.) would invade Poland.

For three weeks the victors of Minsk covered their ten to fifteen miles a day, by-passing without much difficulty at first the units which Field-Marshal Model, like General Weygand after June 11, 1940, threw in piecemeal to stop the gaps. Model, the new C.-in-C. Army Group "Centre", now had the job of holding back the enemy long enough for O.K.H. to regroup its forces and to reform the

indispensable continuous front. He was more highly regarded by Hitler than his unfortunate predecessor, and was thus able to obtain in time permission to evacuate a whole series of so-called "fortified areas" which otherwise would have become so many death-traps for the army's divisions. This meant, of course, considerable sacrifices of territory:

July 13: Chernyakhovsky takes Vilnyus;

July 14: Rokossovsky envelops Pinsk, on the Pripet;

July 15: Chernyakhovsky forces the Niemen at Alytus, while Zakharov takes Grodno;

July 18: Rokossovsky crosses the Russo-Polish frontier fixed at Teheran;

July 23: Rokossovsky's advance guard enters Lublin;

July 27: Zakharov breaks through the defences of Białystok;

July 28: Rokossovsky takes Brest-Litovsk;

July 31: Rokossovsky enters Praga, across the Vistula from Warsaw;

August 1: Chernyakhovsky reaches Kalvariya, 15 miles from the Prussian frontier; and

August 2: Chernyakhovsky takes Kaunas.

On Chernyakhovsky's right, General Bagramyan and the armies of the 1st

▽ *A wounded German officer awaits transport at a dressing station on the Eastern Front. The label gives details of the wound and treatment he has received. The war in Russia had drained Germany of many of its older experienced soldiers, and they were now being replaced by new recruits unversed in battle craft and the skills of survival.*

△ *Soviet troops in position with a 45-mm anti-tank gun.*
▷ *In liberated Vilnyus Russian officers pass a rather more potent tank killer: an 8.8-cm Flak gun and a Volkswagen* Kübelwagen *captured from the Germans.*

▽ *A Russian junior lieutenant with his sergeant check their map during a reconnaissance in a forward position.*

Baltic Front poured through the breaches in the inner flanks of Army Groups "North" and "Centre" caused by the Vitebsk catastrophe. Whilst the means were lacking to stop the enemy's advance towards Riga, was it advisable to keep the German 16th and 18th Armies on the Polotsk–Pskov–Lake Peipus line, which they had been holding since their painful retreat of the preceding winter? Colonel-General Lindemann, C.-in-C. Army Group "North", concluded that it was not and advised the withdrawal of his forces on the left bank of the Dvina. He was also being asked to transfer certain of his units to Army Group "Centre", which strengthened his point of view.

But to abandon Estonia might risk the "defection" of Finland, as O.K.W. put it. And so on July 2 Hitler relieved Lindemann of his command and handed it over to General Friessner, who in February 1944 had distinguished himself as commander of *Armeegruppe* "Narva". This change of personnel did nothing to improve the strategic situation.

On July 11 Bagramyan crossed the Dvina at Drissa and further to the left his advance guard reached Utena in Lithuania. On the following day the 2nd Baltic Front (General A. I. Eremenko) came into the battle and, breaking out from the area of Novosol'niki, drove deep into the positions of the German 16th Army (General Loch).

Caught up in front by Eremenko and behind by Bagramyan, the latter threatening his communications, Friessner, who had had to give up 12 divisions to Model, could only come to the same conclusions on July 12 as his predecessor had done. But, faced with the same refusal from Hitler to meet the situation with common sense, he did not hesitate, at the end of his letter dated that day, to stake his command:

"If, *mein Führer*," he wrote, "you are not prepared to accept my idea and give me the liberty of action necessary to carry out the measures proposed above, I shall be compelled to ask you to relieve me of the responsibilities I have assumed so far." Summoned by return of post to Rastenburg, Friessner upheld his view in the presence of the Führer, who reproached him for having used threats and for having shown an unmilitary attitude throughout. Reminding Hitler that he was responsible for some 700,000 men, and that he was fighting at the relative strength of one to eight, according to the account he has left of this interview he went so far as to say:

"I am not trying to hang on to my job. You can relieve me of it. You can even have me shot if you want to. But to ask me, *in full knowledge of the facts and against the dictates of my conscience,* to lead the men entrusted to me *to certain destruction*–that you can never do."

Hitler, with tears in his eyes, is thereupon supposed to have seized General Friessner's hand and promised him every support. But the facts are that each one stuck to his own position. And so Colonel-General Schörner, C.-in-C. Army Group "South Ukraine", was ordered on July 23 to change places immediately with Friessner, C.-in-C. Army Group "North", who was himself promoted to Colonel-General.

Army Group "North" cut off

Amongst the general officers of the Wehrmacht, Schörner was one of the few who was unswerving in his loyalty to the Führer. However great his National Socialist zeal, however, it was not in his power to satisfy Hitler, for the 3rd Baltic Front (General Maslennikov) now went over to the offensive and extended the battle further northwards. This was followed on July 25 by an attack by the Leningrad Front (Marshal of the U.S.S.R. L. A. Govorov). In all a dozen armies totalling at least 80 divisions took part in this concentric offensive.

▽ *Soviet 76-mm guns on the 2nd Belorussian Front. With a range of over 12,000 yards these guns were the backbone of Soviet field artillery. The heavy losses suffered at the beginning of "Barbarossa" allowed the Russians to start from scratch with the reorganisation and standardisation of their artillery, some of which dated back to before World War I.*

Whilst Govorov was breaking through the Narva defile and Maslennikov, after liberating Pskov on July 21, was also driving on into Estonia, on July 26 Eremenko, anchoring his left flank on the Dvina, captured the towns of Rēzekne (Rositten) and Dvinsk (Daugav'pils) in Latvia. Bagramyan, who was using what Hitler called the "hole in the Wehrmacht", or the still gaping breach between the right and left of Army Groups "North" and "Centre", changed direction from west to north west and, driving through Panevežys, Jelgava (Mittau), and Tukums, reached the Gulf of Riga to the west of the great Latvian port in the evening of August 1. As Generals Lindemann and Friessner had never ceased to predict, Army Group "North", with some 30 divisions, was cut off in Estonia and northern Latvia. More fortunate than Paulus at Stalingrad, however, Schörner could confidently rely on the Baltic for supplies and evacuation, since the Gulf of Finland was blocked right across so that Soviet submarines could not operate in the open sea. In the Gulf of Riga his right flank was efficiently supported by the guns of the German fleet – by the very warships which Hitler had wanted to scrap in 1943.

Konev attacks

On the German side of the immense front line stretching from the Baltic to the Carpathians, the second fortnight in July brought defeat to Army Group "North Ukraine". This added further disaster to the crushing of Army Group "Centre", the last consequences of which were still far from being played out. The tension was such that, taking also into account the American breakthrough in Normandy, it might have been thought that the last hour had struck for the Wehrmacht and for Greater Germany's Third Reich. This was how Marshal Rokossovsky saw events when he stated to a correspondent of the British *Exchange Telegraph* on July 26:

"It is no longer important to capture such and such a position. The essential thing is to give the enemy no respite. The Germans are running to their deaths ... Their troops have lost all contact with their command."

On the following day a spokesman of *Stavka* spoke in the same terms at a press conference: "The Führer's G.H.Q. will no more be able to hold the line of the Vistula than it did those of the Bug and the San. The German Army is irremediably beaten and breaking up."

Also on July 13 Marshal Konev and the forces of the 1st Ukrainian Front had come into the battle, extending the action of the three Belorussian Fronts from the area of Kovel' to the left bank of the Dniestr. According to the Soviet military historian Boris S. Telpukhovsky, whose account we have no reason to doubt, Konev had been given by *Stavka* all the necessary men and *matériel* to secure an easy victory over Army Group "North Ukraine", which was still, together with Army Group "Centre", under the command of Model. For this assault Konev had 16,213 guns and rocket-launchers, 1,573 tanks, 463 assault guns, 3,240 aircraft, and no fewer than seven armies, including the 1st and 3rd Guards Tank Armies and the 4th Tank Army, commanded respectively by Generals M. E. Katukov, P. S. Rybalko, and D. D. Lelyushenko, all three very experienced tank commanders.

On the German side, Army Group "North Ukraine" had had to give up to Army Group "Centre" four Panzer and three infantry divisions since June 22 and was reduced to 43 divisions (of which five were Panzer and one *Panzergrenadier*) and two mountain brigades. Assuming that between April and June the German armoured divisions had been brought up to their normal strength of 160 fighting and command tanks which, knowing the aberrations of Adolf Hitler, seems highly unlikely, the Russians outnumbered them by two to one. In the air Russian superiority was of the order of five to one. Hence the disaster which befell 8th Panzer Division on July 14. Disregarding orders, it took the main road to Brody to speed up its counter-attack. Major-General von Mellenthin writes:

"Eight Panzer was caught on the move by Russian aircraft and suffered devastating losses. Long columns of tanks and lorries went up in flames, and all hope of counterattack disappeared."

Marshal Konev had forces so powerful and so numerous at his command that he could give his offensive two centres of gravity. On the right, in the area southwest of Lutsk, a first group containing notably the 1st Guards Tank Army, was to break up the 4th *Panzerarmee* (General Harpe) then exploit its victory in a general south-west direction. On the

◁ ◁ *The crew of a 15-cm gun proceeds with routine maintenance while their comrades lend a hand with the ploughing.*
△ *Rokossovsky: "It is no longer important to capture such and such a position. The essential thing is to give the enemy no respite. The Germans are running to their deaths ..."*

△ *Schörner, one of Hitler's most fanatically loyal generals – he, too, was given the impossible task of plugging the vast breaches torn open in the German front.*

△ *Illusion. "The Führer is saved!" "Then the secret weapon's failed." (From Götenborg Hand Tidning).*

△ Detroit Star's *cartoonist Burch neatly sums up Hitler's unenviable position: "Between two fires".*

▽ *From Moscow's* Krokodil. *The "Hitlerite hordes" dash themselves to ruin against the rock of the Red Army.*

left a second group, containing the 3rd Guards Tank Army and the 4th Tank Army, had concentrated in the area of Ternopol': attacking due west it was to engage the 1st *Panzerarmee* (Colonel-General Raus) and form a pincer with the first group.

Model retreats

By evening on D-day the German defences in the two sectors were already seriously damaged. On the following day Colonel-General Raus put the 1st and 8th Panzer Divisions under XLVIII Panzer Corps for an eventual counter-attack, but this failed as a result of the circumstances described above by Mellenthin. Twenty-four hours later not only had the Russians broken through at the points previously designated by Konev, but the pincers had closed on General Hauffe's XIII Corps between L'vov and Brody.

And so a new "moving pocket" was formed, from which several thousand men managed to escape during a night-attack of hand-to-hand fighting. On July 23, however, General Hauffe had been taken prisoner together with 17,000 men of his corps and the victors counted 30,000 German corpses on the battlefield.

In the German sectors facing Rokossovsky and Konev, it was Model's intention to re-establish his line along the Bug. This evidently over-optimistic plan came to nothing in view of the weakness of Army Group "Centre" and the recent defeat of Army Group "North Ukraine". Worse still, the breach between the right flank of the 4th *Panzerarmee* and the left flank of the 1st was now wide open and there was the great danger that the latter's communications with Kraków would be cut and that the army would be driven back against the Carpathians. Hence, in full agreement with Colonel-General Guderian, who had succeeded Zeitzler as Chief-of-Staff at O.K.H. after the attempt on Hitler's life on July 20, Model drew back to the line of the Vistula and its extension the San above Deblin.

Even if the Germans, after their defeats of June 22 and July 13, had managed to establish a front line behind these ditches, this last-minute attempt could not have saved the Polish oilwells at Drogobycz and Boryslaw which became a heavy and irreparable loss to the military economy of the Third Reich. The situation between the Narew and the Carpathians was now deteriorating so rapidly that O.K.H. had to draw on the strength of Army Group "South Ukraine" and send four Panzer and seven infantry divisions from Moldavia to Galicia.

The Russians reach the Vistula

Before these reinforcements could be put to use, Marshals Rokossovsky and Konev had reached the Vistula and the San at Blitzkrieg speed, mopping up German columns retreating on foot or in horse-drawn vehicles. Between July 28 and 31, tanks of the 1st Belorussian Front covered the 120 miles between Brest-Litovsk and the suburbs of Warsaw. They also crossed the Vistula at Magnuszew and Pulawy, upstream from the capital. Rokossovsky's optimistic view of events quoted above seems to have been justified. The 1st Ukrainian Front had similar quick successes, covering 125 miles on a front some 250 miles wide on July 27. On that same day its formations on the right got beyond Przemysl on the west bank of the San and cleaned up L'vov on the way, whilst on the left, having crossed the Dniestr, it captured Stanislawow and threw back to the Carpathians the Hungarian 1st and 2nd Armies, which had formed the right flank of Army Group "North Ukraine" since the end of the winter. The situation now looked very dangerous.

A few days later Konev got a bridge-head over 30 miles deep over the Vistula in the area of Sandomierz, drove on beyond the San as far as Rzeszów, more than 90 miles beyond L'vov, and on August 7 occupied the oil wells at Drogobycz and Boryslaw.

Massive losses

A Moscow communiqué dated July 25 put the German losses since the start of the summer offensive at some 60 divisions, or 380,000 killed and more than 150,000 prisoners. The figures seem acceptable. On the other hand, the figure of 2,700 tanks destroyed or captured, as the complement of 17 fully-equipped Panzer divisions, seems unlikely.

The Russian Lavochkin La-7 fighter and fighter-bomber

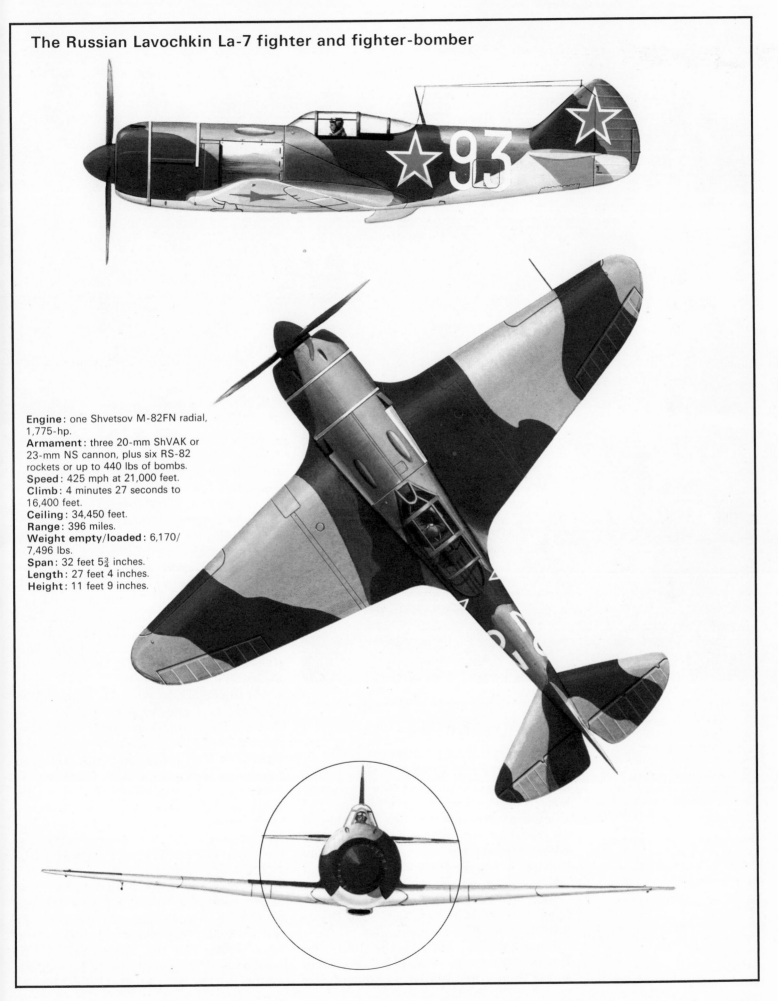

Engine: one Shvetsov M-82FN radial, 1,775-hp.
Armament: three 20-mm ShVAK or 23-mm NS cannon, plus six RS-82 rockets or up to 440 lbs of bombs.
Speed: 425 mph at 21,000 feet.
Climb: 4 minutes 27 seconds to 16,400 feet.
Ceiling: 34,450 feet.
Range: 396 miles.
Weight empty/loaded: 6,170/7,496 lbs.
Span: 32 feet $5\frac{3}{4}$ inches.
Length: 27 feet 4 inches.
Height: 11 feet 9 inches.

△ △ *A 76-mm gun of the 1st Ukrainian Front in action as an anti-tank weapon.*
△ *A Panther tank and a column of trucks overtake bicycle riding infantrymen during the German retreat through Galicia. The bicycle featured throughout the war as a cheap and efficient mode of transport which did not need convoys of petrol tankers. Even towards the end of the war, British airborne troops used a handy collapsible version.*

The retreat halts

From the Dvina at Vitebsk to the Niemen at Kaunas is 250 miles as the crow flies and from the Dniepr at Orsha to the Vistula at Warsaw 400; the bridgehead at Sandomierz reached by Konev's advance guard was over 180 miles from the area of Lutsk. The whole of this rapid advance, carried out on the old cavalry principle of "to the last breath of the last horse and the last horseman" had therefore reached its strategic limit.

Between the Carpathians and the Narew, however, O.K.H.'s reinforcements, though improvised, were beginning to take effect. The 17th Army (General Schulz) filled the gap between the 1st and 4th *Panzerarmee* and the 9th Army (General von Vormann) occupied the left flank of the 4th *Panzerarmee* between the Sandomierz bridgehead and a point downstream of Warsaw. There also came into the battle from the interior or from Moldavia a good half-dozen armoured divisions, including the "Hermann Göring", the S.S. 3rd *"Totenkopf"* and 5th *"Wiking"* Panzer, and the excellent *"Grossdeutschland"* Panzergrenadier. Volume IV of the *Great Patriotic War* gives a good account of this change in the situation of the two sides:

"At the end of July . . . the tempo of the offensive had greatly slowed down. The German High Command had by this time thrown very strong reserves against the main sectors of our advance. German resistance was strong and stubborn. It should also be considered that our rifle divisions and tank corps had suffered heavy losses in previous battles; and the artillery and the supply bases were lagging behind, and that the troops were short of both petrol and munitions.

"Infantry and tanks were not receiving nearly enough artillery support. During the delays in re-basing our air force on new airfields, this was much less active than before. At the beginning of the Belorussian Campaign, we had complete control of the air. At the beginning of

which led to this victory by the Red Army would land the Russians inside the Third Reich.

2. Between June 1 and August 30, 1944, Germany's land forces lost on the Eastern Front alone 916,860 in killed, wounded, and prisoners. The human resources of the Third Reich were therefore rapidly running out and would not be made up by the expedient of "people's grenadier" (Volksgrenadier) divisions.

3. French émigrés returning to their country after the fall of Napoleon were said to have learned nothing and forgotten nothing. Hitler's example shows that one can do worse: he learned nothing and forgot everything. The failure of the attempt on his life on July 20 would therefore allow him to indulge his despotism and incompetence to the full.

4. The fourth and last conclusion comes in the form of a question. The *Great Patriotic War* says that the forces of

▽ *Russian gunners using captured German 10.5-cm guns to supplement the fire of their 76-mm guns in a shoot in the Carpathians. Both sides used captured equipment, from tanks and artillery to boots and small arms.*

August our superiority was temporarily lost. In the 1st Belorussian sector between August 1 and 13 our planes carried out 3,170 sorties and the enemy planes 3,316."

Doubtless, and for reasons which we shall see shortly, these statements by the Soviet writers are not completely impartial. Nevertheless by August 16, the day on which Model was given the job of repairing the situation, the position on the Eastern Front can be said to have stabilised temporarily between Kalvariya and the Carpathians. In particular the 4th *Panzerarmee* and the 9th Army had managed to reduce the bridgeheads at Sandomierz (Baranow), Pulawy, and Magnuszew, but not to eliminate them completely. On the right bank of the Vistula the Soviet 2nd Tank Army suffered a defeat at Wolomin and Radzymin, a few miles from Warsaw, which cost 3,000 killed and 6,000 prisoners together with a considerable amount of *matériel*.

Balance-sheet

This short pause gives us an opportunity to put forward some conclusions on these six weeks of operations on the Eastern Front:

1. Warsaw may be 400 miles from Orsha, but it is only 350 from Berlin. So a repetition of the German mistakes

△ German prisoners in Maidanek concentration camp march past stacks of unrecognisable human remains. The Russians showed the camp to their own soldiers and to Western journalists. Alexander Werth reported that "the Germans went through the camp, at first at an ordinary pace, and then faster and faster, till they ran in a frantic panicky stampede, and they were green with terror, and their hands shook and their teeth chattered."

the 1st Belorussian Front arrived exhausted on the banks of the Vistula, which explains the halt in their advance: but could not *Stavka* have made up its strength with units and *matériel* already earmarked for campaigns in Rumania and Hungary so as to maintain the drive westwards? As we are aware that a theatre of operations can only absorb as many men and as much *matériel* as can be supplied by its means of communication, we leave the last question unanswered.

Warsaw–betrayed?

We are thus brought to the controversy which arose between the West and the Soviets over the behaviour of Stalin, *Stavka,* and the Red Army towards the Warsaw rising started at 1700 hours on August 1 by General Bor-Komorowski, C.-in-C. of the Polish Home Army. We cannot imitate Telpukhovsky, who maintains a prudent silence on this subject but nevertheless devotes a page and a half of his extensive work to the liberation of the little Polish village of Guerasimowichy

on July 26, 1944. In his memoirs, Winston Churchill, reporting the return to Praga of Rokossovsky about September 15, made no bones about the reasons for the tragic episode as he saw them:

"The Russians occupied the Praga suburb, but went no further. They wished to have the non-Communist Poles destroyed to the full, but also to keep alive the idea that they were going to their rescue.

"Such was their liberation of Poland, where they now rule. But this cannot be the end of the story."

Churchill was doubtless writing under the influence of the exchange of telegraph messages he had had with Stalin on the subject of Warsaw, and was remembering the help he had wanted to give by air to the stricken city and its heroic defenders. He did not know then as well as we do now about the operations in the suburbs of the Polish capital between August 1 and 4. Michel Garder, writing in 1961 after carefully researching Soviet material published after 1953, agrees in broad essentials with Churchill. "With Rokossovsky within 32 miles of Warsaw," he writes, "it seemed to General Bor-Komorowski that the arrival of the Russian troops could only be a matter of a few days. It was the duty of the Poles to welcome the Soviets as allies and not as 'liberator-occupiers'. This was just what Stalin did not want.

"In the eyes of the Kremlin, the Polish Home Army was merely a tool of the 'reactionary Polish clique' in London whose leaders, in addition to their 'enslavement to capitalism' and their 'bourgeois chauvinism' had had the effrontery to state that the Katyn massacres were the work of the N.K.V.D.

"Having suddenly run out of steam, the irresistible 1st Belorussian Front offensive had found itself facing the German bridgehead in front of Warsaw. To get so far had, it is true, cost Rokossovsky's armies a great effort. Their lines of communication were stretched. They needed a few days' respite and probably considerable reinforcements in men and *matériel* to bring them back up to strength. But nothing, other than political considerations by the Kremlin, could justify the semi-inertia of the Soviet troops in September when they reached the suburbs of Praga."

Werth is less certain than Churchill or Garder. He seems to give credence to the pessimistic figures for the 1st Belorussian Front on August 1 quoted above from the *Great Patriotic War*. On the other hand, he does not omit the passage which refers to the defeat of the Soviet 2nd Tank Army before Praga, where it was attacked on its left flank by five German divisions, including four Panzer. It is interesting to see that he was personally involved on one occasion. Received in Lublin by Rokossovsky he recorded the following on the spot:

"'I can't go into any details. But I'll tell you just this. After several weeks' heavy fighting in Belorussia and eastern Poland we finally reached the outskirts of Praga about the 1st of August. The Germans, at this point, threw in four armoured divisions, and we were driven back.'

'How far back?'

'I can't tell you exactly, but let's say nearly 100 kilometres (sixty-five miles).'

'Are you still retreating?'

'No—we are now advancing—but slowly.'

'Did you think on August 1 (as was suggested by the *Pravda* correspondent that day) that you could take Warsaw within a very few days?'

'If the Germans had not thrown in all that armour, we could have taken Warsaw, though not in a frontal attack; but it was never more than a 50-50 chance. A German counter-attack at Praga was not to be excluded, though we now know that before these armoured divisions arrived, the Germans inside Warsaw were in a panic, and were packing up in a great hurry.'

'Wasn't the Warsaw Rising justified in the circumstances?'

'No it was a bad mistake. The insurgents started it off their own bat, without consulting us.'

'There was a broadcast from Moscow calling on them to rise.'

'That was routine stuff *(sic)*. There were similar calls to rise from *Swit* radio [Home Army], and also from the Polish service of the BBC—so I'm told, though I didn't hear it myself. Let's be serious. An armed insurrection in a place like Warsaw could only have succeeded if it had been carefully co-ordinated with the Red Army. The question of timing was of the utmost importance. The Warsaw insurgents were badly armed, and the rising would have made sense only if we were already on the point of *entering Warsaw. That point had not been reached*

△ *Soviet sub-machine gunners ford the west Bug river in the Ukraine.*

▽ *A KV-85 roars past the shattered remains of a 3.7-cm anti-tank gun during the fighting before Warsaw.*

△ *Russian prisoners digging an anti-tank trench near Warsaw. Aware of the threat that the large numbers of adults in Warsaw posed to their rear areas, the Germans had plans to evacuate the population of the city.*

at any stage, and I'll admit that some Soviet correspondents were much too optimistic on the 1st of August. We were pushed back. We couldn't have got Warsaw before the middle of August, even in the best of circumstances. But circumstances were not good, but bad. Such things do happen in war. It happened at Kharkov in March 1943 and at Zhitomir last winter.'

'What prospect is there of your getting back to Praga within the next few weeks?'

'I can't go into that. All I can say is that we shall try to capture both Praga and Warsaw, but it won't be easy.'

'But you have bridgeheads south of Warsaw.'

'Yes, but the Germans are doing their damnedest to reduce them. We're having much difficulty in holding them, and we are losing a lot of men. Mind you, we have fought non-stop for over two months now.'"

Whilst accepting the good faith and accuracy of Werth's report, it would seem that it should be interpreted as follows: Rokossovsky and, behind him, the Soviet high command, had well and

truly got over their elation of July 26, and at a distance now of 30 days were claiming never to have felt it. However, at 2015 hours on July 15 Radio Moscow broadcast a stirring appeal to the population of Warsaw and a few hours later the Union of Polish Patriots station, which followed the Soviet line, took up the call:

"The Polish Army now entering Polish territory had been trained in the U.S.S.R. It unites with the People's Army to form the body of the Polish Armed Forces, the backbone of our nation in her struggle for independence. The sons of Warsaw will rally to its ranks tomorrow. Together with the allied army they will drive out the enemy to the west, expel Hitler's vermin from Poland and deal a mortal blow to the remains of Prussian imperialism. For Warsaw which did not yield, but fought on, the hour has struck."

And, as it was to be expected that the enemy, now cornered, would retreat into the capital, the appeal for an uprising continued: "This is why . . . by energetic hand-to-hand fighting in the streets of Warsaw, in the houses, the factories, the warehouses, not only shall we hasten the coming of our final liberation, but we shall safeguard our national heritage and the lives of our brothers."

Stalin stands aloof

On August 5 Churchill sent Stalin a request to intervene on behalf of the insurrectionists, but he was answered by scepticism: Stalin doubted, if not the reality, at least the importance of the uprising.

On August 16, when Churchill repeated his demands, Stalin expressed his conviction that "the Warsaw operation is a horrible and senseless venture which is costing the lives of a great many of the population. This would not have arisen if the Soviet Command had been informed beforehand and if the Poles had kept in constant touch with us."

However, it was not Mikołajczyk's Polish Government-in-Exile which had broken off relations with the Kremlin. Must one therefore assume that Stalin supposed that the Home Army would be deaf to the call to arms given on July 29? Surely not. Be that as it may, this led Stalin to the following conclusion: "From the situation thus created, the Soviet Command deduces that it must dissociate itself from the Warsaw adventure, as it has no responsibility, either direct or indirect, in the operation."

Stalin was not content, however, merely with dissociating himself from the insurrectionists (whom he called on August 22 a "handful of criminals who, in order to seize power, have unleashed the Warsaw venture") but also obstinately refused to allow Anglo-American aircraft to land on Soviet territory in order to refuel from their operations over Warsaw. He knew that this would severely restrict the Allies, who were attempting to fly in supplies to the defenders of the unhappy city.

No help from Roosevelt

Would Stalin eventually have given in to Churchill if Roosevelt had thrown in the weight of his authority? We do not know. What we do know, however, is that on August 26, taking into account the "general perspectives of the war", the American President refused to join

forces with the British Prime Minister in a new approach to Stalin. He was doubtless influenced by Hopkins and Morgenthau. On September 2, James V. Forrestal, who had succeeded Frank Knox (who died on April 28, 1944) as Secretary of the Navy, noted in his diary:

"I find that whenever any American suggests that we act in accordance with the needs of our own security he is apt to be called a god-damned fascist or imperialist, while if Uncle Joe suggests that he needs the Baltic Provinces, half Poland, all Bessarabia and access to the Mediterranean, all hands agree that he is a fine frank, candid and generally delightful fellow who is very easy to deal with because he is so explicit in what he wants."

Warsaw's epic fight

The rest is history. The defenders of Warsaw met their fate with the most sublime heroism. Having driven the Russians back over 30 miles from the right bank of the Vistula, the Germans calmly set about the reconquest of the Polish capital with large numbers of Tiger tanks, assault guns, and little

△ Soviet soldiers move cautiously through a state room of Razdravanu Castle, during the fighting for Iaşi.

▽ Know your enemy: German soldiers examine a captured T-34, taken during the fighting near the Warsaw suburb of Praga.

△ *A section of Russian riflemen moves forward during the fighting in Praga. The right flank of the 1st Belorussian Front reached the suburb on July 31, and the Warsaw Rising began a day later.*
▷ ▷ *Soldiers of the Home Army entering the Telephone Exchange. Though most of their weapons and equipment were of German origin, they displayed the red and white Polish national colours, seen here on their helmets.*

Goliath tanks, a kind of remote-controlled bomb on tracks. The heaviest weapons the defenders had were of 20-mm calibre.

They fought from barricade to barricade, from house to house, from storey to storey and even in the sewers. The area occupied by the defenders gradually shrank, so that the meagre supplies dropped by Anglo-American aircraft fell increasingly into enemy hands. The repression of the uprising was entrusted to Himmler. He appointed *Waffen*-S.S. General von dem Bach-Zalewski and gave him, amongst others, S.S. police units, a brigade of Russian ex-prisoners, and a brigade of ex-convicts, all of whom had committed such excesses that Guderian had persuaded Hitler to remove them from the front.

In the second fortnight of September the Russians reoccupied Praga but remained virtually passive opposite the capital. Under these conditions Bor-Komorowski, who had had 22,000 killed, missing, or seriously wounded out of his 40,000 fighters, resigned himself to surrender on October 2, obtaining from von dem Bach-Zalewski an assurance that his men would without exception be treated under the Geneva Convention of August 27, 1929 governing prisoners-of-war.

Stalin's responsibility

From this brief summary of the essential facts it is possible to conclude:

1. The Warsaw "venture", which aroused the ire and indignation of Stalin, was remotely controlled from Moscow, but without criminal intent.
2. Since the Russians played down as much as possible the defeat of Rokossovsky at Praga, the will to let the Polish Home Army be massacred was imputed to an inertia which arose to a great extent from impotence.
3. Under these conditions it cannot be proved that Anglo-American aircraft taking off from Foggia could have saved the Home Army if Stalin had allowed them to land on Soviet territory.
4. But it can be stated that, by refusing them this permission, Stalin left no alternative to the insurrectionists of August 1 but death or captivity and that he did so knowingly and willingly.

The Poles will never forget.

THE
WARSAW
RISING

1. *A patrol dashes across a street in the opening stages of the Warsaw Rising. As the fighting developed they captured uniforms and equipment and began to look like a regular army.*
2. *A German vehicle captured in the early days.*
3. *After nearly a month of fighting the Home Army stormed the "Pasta" Telephone Exchange, one of the German strongpoints. Here prisoners taken on August 20 emerge from the battered building.*

"Soldiers of the capital! I have today issued the order which you desire, for open warfare against Poland's age-old enemy, the German invader. After nearly five years of ceaseless and determined struggle, carried on in secret, you stand today openly with arms in hand, to restore freedom to our country, and to mete out fitting punishment to the German criminals for the terror and crimes committed by them on Polish soil."

With these words General Bor-Komorowski, Commander-in-Chief of the Polish Home Army, proclaimed the Warsaw Rising of August 1, 1944. With the guns of the Red Army already audible on the eastern bank of the Vistula, it seemed indeed that the long-awaited moment had come to rid the Polish capital of its German overlords.

"With arms in hand"–that was the rub, for there were precious few of them. Aid from outside was essential, but at the outset it was considered inevitable. The insurgents counted on aid from the Red Army–and from the long air arm of the Western Allies. But international power politics intervened, and the men and women of Warsaw were left on their own.

No account of the Warsaw Rising, no matter how objective, can ignore this fact. In telling the story for later generations one returns, time and again, to the unmitigated heroism of an army which fought, like the French at Waterloo, "without fear and without hope".

Hope, certainly, was not lacking in the first week of the Rising.

But by August 8 an inevitable note of anxiety, of perplexity, was beginning to infuse the despatches from the stricken city:

"**August 2.** We have inflicted very heavy and bloody losses in men and motorised equipment on the enemy; we have taken prisoners. We are afraid of nothing except a shortage of ammunition . . .

"**August 3.** The initiative is in our hands. German morale has been greatly undermined . . .

"**August 5.** At present our offensive weakens in proportion to our expenditure of ammunition . . . Since yesterday morning there has been complete silence on the other side of the Vistula.

"**August 6.** I have to state that in her present struggle Warsaw is getting no aid from the Allies, just as Poland got no aid in 1939

4. *General Bor-Komorowski, C.-in-C. of the Polish Home Army.*
5. *General Tadeusz Pełczyński or "Grzegorz", Bor's deputy and chief-of-staff.*
6. *A captured German half-track personnel carrier, clearly marked with a Polish eagle.*
7. *Polish soldiers receive a lecture in the field on reloading the 7.62 DP light machine gun.*
8. *A patrol of the Polish Kosciuszko Division in the fighting on the outskirts of the city. When elements of this unit, which was attached to the Red Army, penetrated the suburbs, they were heavily attacked by the Germans.*

4

5

8

6

7

1811

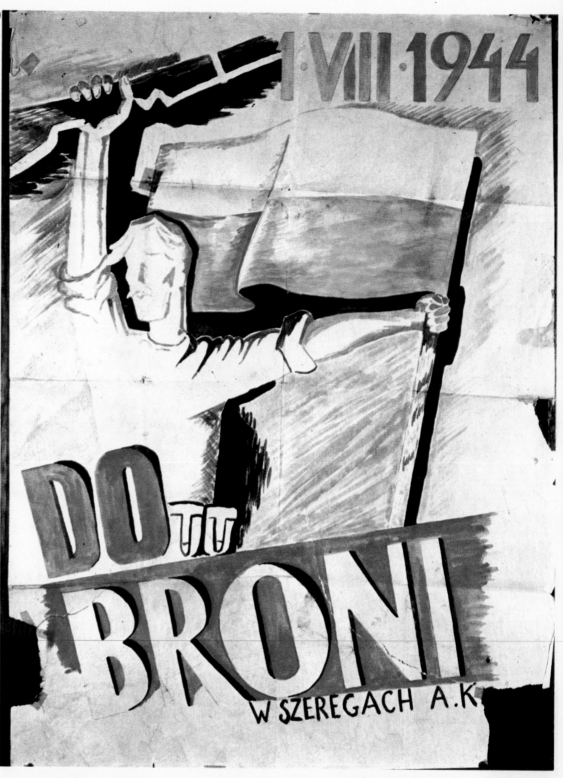

Warsaw's fight aroused the admiration of the world but inspired far too little in the way of practical aid.

9. *A typical example—an English poster which was of as much effective use as the placards of 1938 urging the British to "Stand by the Czechs".*

10. *"To Arms!"—poster calling the Warsaw Home Army forces to begin the Rising.*

11. *Moscow's myth: Warsaw's prison bars, shattered by the joint efforts of the Red Army and the Polish units fighting under its aegis.*

. . . but even if the situation were to become critical, none the less we should go on fighting . . .

"**August 8.** We have almost completely lost any possibility of aggressive action, owing to our remaining ammunition being used up . . .

"**August 10.** A German leaflet entitled 'ultimatum' calls on the population to leave the city in a westerly direction. From the Soviet side—silence . . . You must positively bomb us today and tomorrow and under cover of it drop maximum supplies at the points indicated . . .

"**August 12.** Today again no supplies although the night was fine; we are exasperated; we are exasperated; we demand a greater effort . . .

"**August 15.** Our possession of the town hall makes it impossible for the enemy to use the route through Theatre Square . . . Your Air Force's effort has made it possible for us to continue the struggle. Fighting Warsaw sends the heroic airmen words of grati-tude and appreciation. We bow our heads before the fallen . . .

"**August 19.** In the Old Town from morning until 1900 hrs. this was our worst day in regard to air bombing, artillery, and mortar bombardment . . .

"**August 21.** A company from the S.S. Cadet School in Poznan called up in the early days of August is taking part in the fight. The enemy's crushing technical superiority has severely tested the resistance of our soldiers and the people . . .

12. *The exhilaration of the early days. Volunteers of the Home Army swear the oath of loyalty.*
13. *In a devoutly religious nation the Church played an important part in the Rising. A priest conducts Mass on August 15, the "Day of the Soldier" commemorating the Battle of the Vistula.*
14. *Altar boys, now messengers in the Home Army, attending Mass at a school in Powiśle. Overleaf: "Houses and soldiers", B. W. Linke's tribute to the soldiers and citizens of Warsaw.*

14

15

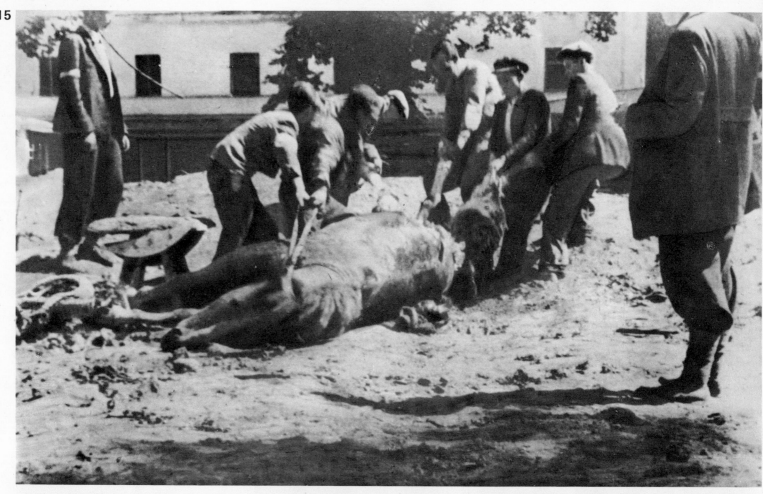

15. *A horse slaughtered for food* **16**
is dragged away to be cut up
by members of the Home Army.
As conditions grew worse
rationing was introduced in the
city.
16. *A medical team lift a*
wounded soldier onto a
stretcher. Though there were
qualified doctors and staff, the
Poles suffered from a shortage
of supplies and equipment.

17. *Colonel Antoni Chrusciel*
("Monter"), commander of the
Warsaw city district.

17

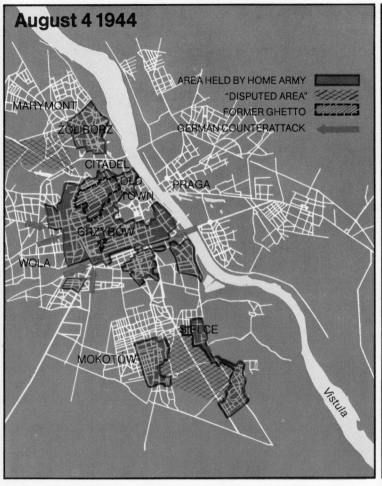

August 4 1944

AREA HELD BY HOME ARMY
"DISPUTED AREA"
FORMER GHETTO
GERMAN COUNTERATTACK

MARYMONT
ŻOLIBORZ
CITADEL
OLD TOWN
PRAGA
GRZYBÓW
WOLA
SIELCE
MOKOTÓW
Vistula

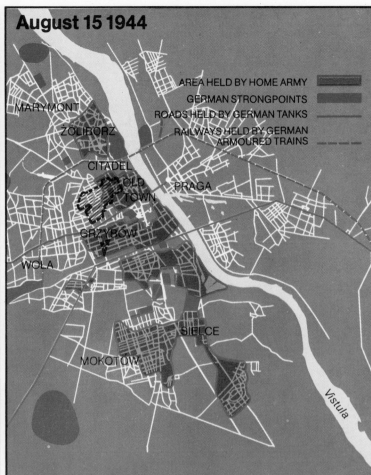

August 15 1944

AREA HELD BY HOME ARMY
GERMAN STRONGPOINTS
ROADS HELD BY GERMAN TANKS
RAILWAYS HELD BY GERMAN ARMOURED TRAINS

MARYMONT
ŻOLIBORZ
CITADEL
OLD TOWN
PRAGA
GRZYBÓW
WOLA
SIELCE
MOKOTÓW
Vistula

"**August 28.** We are now fighting for the 28th day in Warsaw. Our situation in the Old Town is difficult. We are stubbornly holding on . . .

"**August 30.** OLD TOWN: Gradual and steady loss of terrain together with the shortage of food, to some extent of water, and the desperate sanitary conditions is causing a more and more serious condition . . .

"**September 3.** Organised detachments coming to the relief of Warsaw were disarmed by Soviet forces on 28.8.44. Please intervene . . .

"**September 5.** We have again changed the seat of our headquarters. Since yesterday there has been no water or electricity in any part of the city . . .

"**September 9.** A hopeless situation. We are losing extensive terrain, we are being compressed into smaller and smaller islands . . . The receipt of powerful and immediate help by bombing and dropping of supplies will prolong our defence. Without that we must capitulate . . .

"**September 15.** During the night of 14th/15th supplies were dropped and received: a few automatic pistols and six mortars . . . after occupying Marymont the enemy rounded up the civil population and shot them . . .

"**September 20.** Wireless liaison with the Soviet Army of Rokossovsky in Praga has been established. On the western side of the Vistula a Soviet force of one battalion has landed on the bank. Contact effected.

"**September 26.** The food situation for both forces and civilians is catastrophic . . . the Rising is breaking down for lack of food . . .

"**September 30.** Our struggle is in its last agony. Today we need mainly food and equipment. Only an immediate blow by the Soviets against Warsaw can save us . . ."

"**October 1.** Warsaw has no longer any chance of defence. I have decided to enter into negotiations for surrender with full combatant rights, which the Germans fully recognise. Negotiations tomorrow . . .

"**October 4.** I report that in fulfilment of the capitulation agreement, which I concluded on 2nd inst., the troops fighting in Warsaw will lay down their arms today and tomorrow . . .

"The conduct of our troops is irreproachable. It arouses the admiration of the enemy. Tadeusz Komorowski, Lieutenant-General."

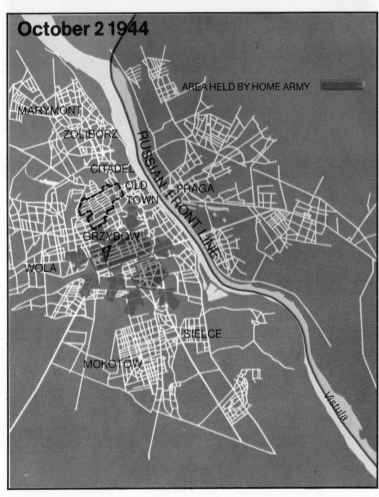

October 2 1944

AREA HELD BY HOME ARMY

MARYMONT
ŻOLIBORZ
CITADEL
OLD TOWN
PRAGA
RUSSIAN FRONT LINE
GRZYBÓW
WOLA
SIELCE
MOKOTÓW
Vistula

18

19

20

18. *With faces drawn by the strain of the intense fighting, a group of civilians emerges from a ruined building.*
19. *Soldiers of the Home Army with P.I.A.T. anti-tank weapons dropped to them by the R.A.F.*
20. *Parachutes stream from weapons containers in a daylight drop by the U.S. Air Force. Near the end of the fighting the Americans made the biggest supply drop of the battle but, tragically, by then it was too late.*
21. *Barricades and shell-damaged buildings in Kredytowa Street. The Germans used tanks, demolition vehicles, and aircraft in their attacks on Polish strongpoints.*
22. *Exhausted and wounded: a group of soldiers captured in October.*

23. *As General Bor-Komorowski* **24** *prepares to enter a car, his Chief of Intelligence, Colonel Iranek-Osmecki shakes hands with General von dem Bach. The Germans permitted the officers to retain their swords after the surrender.*

24. *A salute is fired over the graves of members of the Home Army.*

25. *Defeated, but not broken, the surviving members of the Army march proudly out of Warsaw with their colours flying and wearing their national armbands.*

25